Essential Primary History

Essential Primary History

Christopher Russell

Open University Press

Open University Press
McGraw-Hill Education
8th Floor
338 Euston Road
London
NW1 3BH

email: enquiries@openup.co.uk
world wide web: www.openup.co.uk

and Two Penn Plaza, New York, NY 10121-2289, USA

First published 2016

A catalogue record of this book is available from the British Library

ISBN-13: 978-0-33-526190-1
ISBN-10: 0-33-526190-6
eISBN: 978-0-33-526191-8

Library of Congress Cataloging-in-Publication Data
CIP data applied for

Typeset by SPi Global

Printed and bound by CPI Group (UK) Ltd, Croydon, CR0 4YY

Praise for this book

"An essential and inspirational guidebook for the successful teaching of history within the primary classroom! If you are in any way involved with the teaching of history, you owe it to yourself to read this book. A 'must have' for all history coordinators and teachers within the primary sector, from trainees to the experienced, who wish to raise the profile of history within their school. Closely tied to the new primary curriculum, it is enriched with excellent ideas to make history in the classroom a fun and memorable experience."
Julia Wilson, Primary Teacher, Hensingham Primary School, UK

"This book is easy to read and will enable all teachers (whatever their stage of career development) to become even better at teaching History. The chapter about the history of the curriculum is particularly interesting because it helps us all to understand what has influenced curriculums and pedagogies over time, whereas the Planning, Assessment and Toolkit chapters are useful on a more practical level. What is particularly ideal for trainee teachers is the Theory into Practice chapter that blends the pedagogy of History with learning theory. I will certainly be recommending this text to all my student teachers."
Maggie Webster, Senior Lecturer and RE Subject Coordinator,
Edge Hill University, UK

"Chris Russell has provided a gem of a guide with lots of practical advice for the student and practising teacher of history in the primary classroom, as well as a good book to read in its own right."
Marian Hodgson, St. Philip's Primary School, Sefton, UK

Dedication

To Sarah, Mum and Dad

Contents

Acknowledgements

I would like to acknowledge the contributions, support and cooperation of the following people: Jennifer Churchill, Katie McGhee, Laura McMinn, Sam Shimmin, Martha Russell (no relation) and Emma Wedgewood.

1

What is history and why is it important?

To teach history effectively it is essential to have a deep understanding as to what history is and why it is important to the development of children. This chapter sets out to explore the unique characteristics of the subject of history and how these convey themselves in the primary classroom. This chapter also explores why the essence of history is an important part of our primary school education and an important factor in developing the whole child.

The starting point for our discussion is 'what is history?' as without a clear definition and understanding of this, how can we determine what is appropriate in primary school history and, furthermore, how can we best set about teaching it?

What is history?

Let's start by thinking of history in its simplest form. One way we can think of history is as *people, places and the past*, which we can call the three Ps. With these terms we can see history as a story of what happened, to whom it happened and where it happened.

History can be many things. On one level, the answer to the question 'what is history?' could simply be a block of time, for example 'the Tudors'. This is not inaccurate: history is indeed made up of blocks of time, and in this way British history can be viewed as divided up into small sections. This can be seen quite clearly in the current history curriculum as well as in previous incarnations of the primary history curriculum.

So history is all the events that have ever occurred throughout time, from the coronations of kings and queens to what you had for breakfast this morning. Some events, however, are deemed to be more significant than others, perhaps for cultural, political or social reasons. This is evident in the primary history curriculum, where the word 'significant' is attributed to individuals, events and turning points in history.

'Aspects of history' is the phrase I use to describe each of the facets of history, or descriptors, for instance, change, the past, bias, skills, identity. Together these are the elements of what history is all about.

However, defining history is a lot more complicated than this. We need to think of history in two ways: the content of history (or what we might refer to as 'subject knowledge') and the process of history (the process of finding out about the past).

We might see history in terms of knowledge and understanding. Knowledge concerns itself with the facts about a period that one might learn. We might know, for instance, that the Romans invaded Britain on three occasions, and we might know the years for those invasions as being 55 BC, 54 BC and AD 43. However, surface-level knowledge can be supported by an underlying understanding of events. Therefore, our knowledge of the Roman invasions can go deeper than just knowing the dates; we might consider the trade possibilities, the search for raw materials and the need for a show of strength at home that could be sated with a military victory.

When we think of history lessons in school, one view might be of a teacher drily asking questions of their class. Questioning is undoubtedly an important part of what history is, and it would be odd if teachers did not ask the children in their class questions about the topic they are covering. However, the process of asking questions itself needs to be considered as a two-way process. Part of the aim of good history teaching is to develop pupils' ability to ask questions as well as answer them. I mean this not only in the literal way – to ask historically valid questions – but also in a holistic way, in that we wish to produce inquisitive minds and children who are curious by nature about the world around them and the adventures of the past. This helps ensure that as future adults they are equipped to ask questions that help them make sense of their world and the people and events that went before. In this way, then, we can see questioning as a skill.

Enquiry, therefore, as advocated by Cooper (2012), the inaugural Schools History Project of March 2014[1] and other sources throughout the years, is at the very heart of what history is. This is a point that has been further reiterated in the 2014 primary national curriculum. Enquiry is thus the 'beating heart' of primary school history and the ability to find out about the past by examining, questioning and reasoning is an essential process of the historian, whether they are a university lecturer or a Year 4 pupil. The aims of the curriculum highlight that children should 'understand the methods of historical enquiry, including how evidence is used rigorously to make historical claims, and discern how and why contrasting arguments and interpretations of the past have been constructed' (Department for Education (DfE), 2013).

The power of evidence cannot be underestimated either. Finding proof, disproving an assertion or supporting an idea is an essential aspect of enquiry and therefore primary history. The concept of provenance is especially important. Having proof that something happened is particularly powerful. Having proof that something happened near where you live is arguably even more powerful and links to ideas of identity and belonging. Evidence provides the opportunity to analyse findings and provide a reasoned explanation for events and decisions of the past. However, there comes a point when certainty becomes more of an issue of probability, an educated guess, when even evidence pointing towards a certain date or event, cannot confirm our thoughts for sure. Once children get the hang of asking questions and being inquisitive, you will be amazed how many questions about history they can ask that have no definitive answer.

Another aspect of history that forms a large part of primary history is that of empathy. The word 'empathy' does not appear in the 2014 curriculum. However, it is unlikely that many teachers will plan a scheme of work that does not involve some 'historical imagining'. It is likely that teachers will ask their children to consider 'how they would feel' if they were in a certain situation. This can be used extremely effectively to

[1]http://www.history.org.uk/news/news_2013.html

encourage children to think about how a protagonist in a particular event felt and perhaps to gain an understanding as to why they acted as they did. 'Hot seating' or 'freeze framing' activities, where children consider the actions of the people of the past, their feelings and motivation, are examples of ways to engage children in their history topic and a means of assessing their developing knowledge of the events being studied.

Understanding, as well as knowledge, can also be seen as an important aspect of what history is. For example, most people will know that the Battle of Hastings was in 1066. However, fewer people will understand the events that led up to the circumstances of Battle of Hastings. Understanding also refers to the way in which we view events from the past. We may view events sympathetically, with an 'understanding' of the conditions and time and the plight of the people, or we may view events with an element of tolerance for views held at that time that might not be in line with our outlook on life today. In this way, understanding can be seen as a historical skill. If we consider exploring an artefact and eliciting as much information as we can from it, we do so with our own views and prejudices in place. Our understanding of the world is informed by our experiences of it. A fashionable brooch, such as that in Figure 1.1, made in the 1920s from a dead animal and with the feet still intact, is somewhat repulsive to us and our twenty-first-century sensibilities, but would have been a status symbol to the young socialite to whom it once belonged. Our understanding of change, such as this example in the field of fashion, is also an important part of what history is.

Therefore, change and continuity, as well as similarities and differences, make up our understanding of what history is. Sometimes, this might be wrapped up in child-friendly language, such as 'then and now'. Your lessons may well focus upon identifying similarities and differences, but identifying differences alone is not history in itself. As a good practitioner, you will want to develop a more analytical approach, so that a child that can begin to reason and explain how they know something and not just that they can identify differences. Therefore, providing opportunities for children to develop such skills and conceptual understanding of history along with the ability to reason and explain can be added to our wider definition of history.

Chronological understanding is an important part of understanding what history is. Developing a 'coherent knowledge and understanding of Britain's past and that of the wider world' (DfE, 2013) through sequencing events and artefacts and developing an understanding of a 'chronological narrative, from the earliest times to the present

Figure 1.1 Brooch

Figure 1.2 A 1925 camera

day' (DfE, 2013) is a crucial element of our history lessons in school. Using a simple everyday artefact from the past, which might not have any particular connection to an era or period being studied, can be explored in order to develop aspects of history. An old camera, for instance, as shown in Figure 1.2, can be used to address skills of observation, questioning, developing vocabulary and sequencing as well as how historical concepts and conceptual understanding can be developed within lessons. This will be developed further in Chapter 3.

As we have seen, people of the past had their own thoughts and ideas, and these may or may not correspond to how we might feel and act today. The idea that someone may hold values and ideals that differ from our own is important for us to acknowledge and understand. There can be reasons for such differences in ideas, as we will explore later, but an important aspect of studying history is the ability to respect and tolerate those differences, whether they be cultural, religious, societal or economic factors.

Recognising that people can hold different points of view is a valuable aspect of history. Just as two children will argue over a dispute during a playground game, history is full of examples of one event being viewed in different ways by different groups of people. The 1966 World Cup final between England and West Germany provides us with a neat analogy here. Geoff Hurst's shot famously hit the crossbar and bounced back down to the ground. To English eyes the ball certainly went in, whilst West German eyes saw the ball bounce away from the goal. Both sets of players saw what they wanted to see, as did the fans in the stadium and those watching at home, based upon their allegiances. The goal stood and hence the history books show that Hurst scored a hat-trick that day and that England won the World Cup. The West Germans were aghast. However, the two sets of supporters will probably never agree. Only one event actually happened, but there are two versions of what happened. Understanding that two versions of an event can exist is essential in developing inquisitive learners. As we have already seen, questioning itself is a skill that lies at the heart of history.

This leads us to the possibility of thinking about historical events in different ways by looking at the same event through a particular lens. In this way, history can be thought of in terms of different types of history – for instance, children's history, black history or women's history. We know for certain that the Second World War, for example, took place and we may study it at school, but we can also look at it through the lens of, say, children's history. What was it like to be a child during the Second World War? In this way, significant events are reviewed in the context of what role children played in the war. In a similar way, history can be portrayed as local history or family history. In recent years, an explosion of history-themed TV programmes has resulted in the emergence of another type of history – popular history.

History is sometimes viewed as an entity that informs our lives today. We might refer to the impact of historical events upon our lives. It is possible to consider the direct impact that actions of the past have on us. We could list many aspects of society and modern life that would be different had events in the past not taken place or had different outcomes. Here we could consider such things as democracy, the justice system, language, land ownership and country borders. At this point we can also consider 'learning from the past' and 'warnings from history' as aspects of history. Equally, we can consider the idea that history is all around us. This is certainly true, since you only need to look at a coin from your pocket to see the motto 'REG FD' or 'REG FID DEF' which refers to the honour *Fidei Defensor* bestowed upon Henry VIII by Pope Leo X in 1521 for Henry's book *Defence of the Seven Sacraments*. This title describes Henry as 'Defender of the Faith' in light of the rise of Martin Luther in central Europe. Despite the changes that would occur only a few years later, Henry VIII kept the title and to this day it is represented on every coin issued by the Royal Mint.

In thinking about history in primary schools, perhaps one of the most important documents is the national curriculum itself. It could be argued that, at least in terms of eras and periods to be studied, the curriculum document defines what history is. Within this document, we can see that the teaching of primary history 'should inspire pupils' curiosity to know more about the past' and 'should equip pupils to ask perceptive questions, think critically, weigh evidence, sift arguments, and develop perspective and judgement'. Equally, 'history helps pupils to understand the complexity of people's lives, the process of change, the diversity of societies and relationships between different groups, as well as their own identity and the challenges of their time' (DfE, 2013). Children working in Key Stage 1

> should develop an awareness of the past, using common words and phrases relating to the passing of time. They should know where the people and events they study fit within a chronological framework and identify similarities and differences between ways of life in different periods. They should use a wide vocabulary of everyday historical terms. They should ask and answer questions, choosing and using parts of stories and other sources to show that they know and understand key features of events. They should understand some of the ways in which we find out about the past and identify different ways in which it is represented. (DfE, 2013)

Similarly, Key Stage 2 pupils

> should continue to develop a chronologically secure knowledge and understanding of British, local and world history, establishing clear narratives within and across the periods they study. They should note connections, contrasts and trends over time and develop the appropriate use of historical terms. They should regularly address and sometimes devise historically valid questions about change, cause, similarity and difference, and significance. They should construct informed responses that involve thoughtful selection and organisation of relevant historical

information. They should understand how our knowledge of the past is constructed from a range of sources. (DfE, 2013)

The ability to organise relevant historical information can also refer to how the children will communicate their new knowledge and what they will do with it. This links to synthesis, in which the children can assimilate new knowledge into their understanding of the world.

We also need to consider aspects of history such as interpretation, perception and bias. Do accounts of the past alter? Can our understanding of an event change? What factors determine how we respond to and feel about events? These are all key questions for you to address when thinking about primary school history. Our perceptions of things are directly influenced by our understanding of now. It is likely that many readers would be uncomfortable if a swastika were hung in a shopping centre now. However, up until the 1930s, a swastika held no negative connotations and was, in some cultures, a symbol of luck. It is our perception that has altered as a result of the meaning that this emblem has come to represent.

There is the opportunity to explore the concept of historiography here. Historiography is the study of the study of history. This incorporates the idea that perceptions can alter and change over time without the introduction of any new evidence, as in the case of the swastika or the fashion brooch we discussed earlier. An elegant, well-to-do lady of the 1920s may well have worn a fox stole to a fashionable restaurant or for an evening at the theatre. Today, with our twenty-first-century views, this is not a widespread fashion statement. As you can see from these examples, time itself, and a shift in commonly held values and attitudes, has caused a change in our perceptions. However, sometimes, new evidence will result in a similar impact. For example, Lance Armstrong was seen as a champion in both the sporting sense and for his work in raising awareness of testicular cancer. He was a hero in many people's eyes until revelations about how he achieved his record seven Tour de France wins came to light. Now the legacy of Lance Armstrong is at best tarnished and, for many people, he can only ever be perceived as a cheat.

Another example in modern times is that of the Hillsborough disaster. To some, the headlines of certain newspapers proclaiming the 'truth' and the words and actions of members of parliament cemented a view of how Liverpool supporters had acted and behaved on that day, as well as protecting the actions of the police and certain individuals within the police. However, with the revelations of the Hillsborough panel led by the Rt. Rev. James Jones, the then Bishop of Liverpool, and the subsequent inquiry, these widely held 'truths' have been exposed and a new understanding of events of that fateful day has been revealed.

When thinking about history, one aspect that can easily be overlooked is that of identity. This area ties history to the human experience. History has strong links to the sense of belonging that people hold. Here, history shares elements with its humanities companions, geography and religious education. A sense of identity can be brought about through the study of our shared past. Walking the streets of a town or city and knowing of what and who went before provides a strong sense of identity and can stir thoughts of civic pride and rekindle passions of pride for your home town. We saw earlier how our interpretations of events are formed and those strongly held beliefs come to a large extent from our backgrounds. A sense of belonging can be developed through a local study unit, whereby the children discover the stories of their neighbourhood and the stories of their own past.

Our thoughts about history are further shaped by other factors. For instance, another level to this understanding concerns the filters through which we experience the world. These can be societal influences, cultural perspectives, religious beliefs and economic considerations. Even geography can influence our thoughts and perceptions of events or people. These are influenced by our prejudices and predilections based upon our personal held beliefs. In the UK, this may be seen through a perceived North–South divide or by local rivalries. An example of this could be the innocent cream tea, which can stir such feelings of pride among Devonians and the Cornish, determined, so I am led to believe, by whether the cream is spread before the jam or after. A Devonshire cream tea consists of the cream being applied first, followed by the jam, whereas for a cream tea to be considered Cornish, the jam needs to be applied first, followed by the cream. To a hungry tourist from another part of the country, with no real link to that part of the world, the differences might be dismissed as quaint or humorous, but to the locals of these counties the difference, no matter how subtle, is of the upmost importance. Such rivalries exist across the country and within other countries too.

Similarly, the rivalry between Manchester and Liverpool is often portrayed as being solely about footballing prowess. But while that may be true, the rivalry goes much further into the past than encounters on the football pitch. The phrase 'Liverpool gentlemen and Manchester men' not only refers to the personal characteristics of each native but is also derived from the activities that took place in each city. Manchester men were used to hard toil, industry and the processes of manufacture, working in dirty conditions, whilst Liverpool gentlemen built their success on commerce, shipping, insurance, trade, and customs and excise. The building of the Manchester Ship Canal in 1887 fuelled the rivalry. Annoyed at the perceived high charges imposed by Liverpool Docks, Mancunians set about finding a means of bypassing the Liverpool docks completely. The Manchester Ship Canal meant that Manchester industry could thrive, with damaging consequences for the Port of Liverpool. Such is the impact of this event that the badges of both Manchester United and Manchester City football clubs depict a ship. This example also demonstrates how aspects of history, such as cause and effect, can be addressed in the classroom. In America there is a rivalry between the west coast and the east coast, while Australia's residents of the cities of Melbourne and Sydney pride themselves on the virtues of their respective home towns based upon the settlement of the land and the original inhabitants against the cultural and global recognition, with the same sense of superiority as exhibited by Mancunians and Liverpudlians.

To understand such cultural or economic rivalries it is clear that we need to see the connection between such feelings and our sense of history. Similarly, such understanding of communities, trades, achievements and people of the past can lead to understanding, tolerance, assimilation and social cohesion.

So far, then, we have explored the question 'what is history?' and discovered that it is an eclectic mix of aspects, as depicted in the mind map of Figure 1.3. That is to say, history comprises what is to be studied as well as the aspects of history that have been revealed in this chapter. These aspects of history, rather than existing as a random mass of individual items, can be collected together and considered as historical

Figure 1.3 Mind map

skills, historical concepts, and attitudes and values. Over the years, other authors have provided their own interpretation as to the nature of history. Turner Bisset (2005), for example, provides an interesting structure of history, using a diagram first produced by the Historical Association in 2001. Using this as a starting point, I have collated the many aspects of history that have been discussed in this chapter and provided a series of illustrations including a table (Table 1.1) which is designed to help you process the many and varied aspects of history.

Without a thorough understanding of these aspects of history, you would merely be paying lip service to the subject and depriving learners of the opportunity to develop a deep sense and understanding of history. With a better understanding of these aspects of history, we can see how skills, such as sequencing, have direct links to other aspects of history, such as concepts and chronology. Similarly, we can see the links between the historical skill of understanding and the attitudes of tolerance and empathy. The skill of questioning matches the attitude of curiosity also cited in the national curriculum document. In 'doing' history, the children develop their deeper understanding of the era being taught as well as the subject and discipline of history itself.

Why is history important?

Now that we have a better understanding of what history is, our thoughts can turn towards thinking about why history is important and why history holds an essential place in the curriculum. So, why is history important? It can be seen as a mirror reflecting

Table 1.1 Skills, concepts, and attitudes and values

Historical skills	Historical concepts	Attitudes and values
Observation	Chronology	Empathy
Sequencing	Change	Tolerance
Questioning	Continuity	Curiosity
Understanding	Similarities	Enthusiasm
Enquiry	Differences	Interest
	'Oldness'	Understanding of different points of view
	Evidence	
	Interpretation	
	Identity	

to us the journey that we, as a civilisation, took to get here, and it also determines our understanding of the world we live in today, from our perceptions of other people and places in the world, to the words and phrases we use in our everyday speech. Our freedom and lifestyle, which we sometimes take for granted, are shaped by our past.

For children the benefits from the study of the past are considerable. Children begin to form a historical understanding almost from the moment they are born. Their view of the world is informed by their everyday encounters, which may include their family and then a wider range of contacts that expands as they get older. Even bedtime stories that begin with the phrase 'once upon a time' allude to a bygone age, helping to create a sense of time. Historical understanding will further develop with television, books, internet, school and computer games that will all inform their emerging understanding of the past, as will familiarity with war memorials, street names and other influences in their local area as well as the family stories, anecdotes and family traditions. This is a common theme in developing historical understanding, as advocated by both Hoodless (2008) and Cooper (2012).

The role of history can be seen as being much more than just learning the stories of days gone by. The subject of history can develop the whole child in terms of their cultural, religious, societal and economic understanding. Although this could be argued for all foundation subjects, history is unique in providing opportunities to go beyond the usual priorities of English, maths and science to uncover a world that is rich with human stories, mistakes and achievements. As discussed earlier in this chapter, history is not just about the units being studied but consists of many aspects of history, including questioning. Developing this faculty, providing opportunities to promote questioning, and challenging children to query evidence rather than allowing them to accept details as 'facts' at face value together constitute one of the most important values of history that adds to the whole child and underlines the importance of the subject.

History is also important because, as we have seen, the subject covers a vast array of aspects. The study of history develops an understanding of society as a whole, it helps promote and develop a holistic child in terms of oneself and a metacognitive awareness of oneself and one's place in the world. It helps create an understanding of relationships between subjects and other areas of learning as well as deepening an appreciation of the wider world in terms of cultural experiences and recognising the significance of events that our happening in our world today. Hoodless (2008) argues that knowledge and understanding of our own history has always been particularly important to the rulers of civilisations across the world in understanding the significance of events and their own place in history.

When we switch on the television and watch the news today, we are tuning into the latest development in a long-running story that was originally set in the past. There are many lead characters, some having already made their exits. In this way, we can begin to understand the allegiances displayed between countries during, for example, the voting for the Eurovision Song Contest or the fraught football rivalries that are displayed between particular countries or teams. Our recognition of these undercurrents can inform how we operate in the modern world. We touched upon social cohesion earlier and the inclusion of the *Baghdad AD 900* study unit in the latest primary history curriculum can be seen as a valuable opportunity for schools to develop aspects such as tolerance and understanding and indeed social cohesion as a whole.

Another commonly held view of the importance of history is that we, as a people, can learn from the past. An often cited example is the desire to avoid war and promote peace. One would imagine that this is hard to argue with and that every right-minded individual would indeed prefer peace to war. However, there seems little evidence to suggest that any real progress has been made in this area or even whether any querulous parties find it in their best interests to halt their activities in order to achieve peace. It seems we are doomed to continually repeat ourselves. However, with the background knowledge and understanding that the study of history gives us, we, as a civilisation, are at least advanced enough and informed enough to know we are repeating ourselves and that there is the potential to avoid this unfortunate consequence.

The fact that we believe we can learn from history not to repeat the mistakes of the past is perhaps an indication of the value and store that we place on the subject in the first place. History does hold a particularly special place in the hearts and minds of people. You only need to read the uproar that surrounds any suggestion of a new curriculum to see how preciously the subject and the study of history can be viewed.

I would argue that the importance that has been placed upon the subject of history can be explained by our most formative experiences. Our understanding of the world, from the moment we are born, is formed by our immediate experiences. For most people, they come from our nuclear family unit. We are told about the world from close-knit sources that promote certain ideals and truths they hold dear and instil in us our own belief systems and a growing, shared understanding of the world.

Of course, some people rebel and shake off these belief systems as soon as they are old enough; others, however, hold them close to their hearts, often without question. In this way family traditions develop and are held in great esteem, and people can become over-protective and guarded if their beliefs are called into question or chal-lenged. These traditions themselves can become merged with other family traditions when you meet and share traditions with partners and create new families. An example of this is 'letting in the New Year', or 'first footing' as it is sometimes known. Growing up, letting in the New Year involved the first visitor entering the house carrying fuel, food, drink and money. Upon entry, everyone was greeted with a 'Happy New Year' and a toast would be made. However, my wife's household celebrated New Year in a slightly different way. The person who let in the New Year had first to leave the house by the back door before midnight and knock on the front door to re-enter after midnight. There was no mention of food, fuel, drink or money. Today, the two traditions have merged to form one new tradition that encompasses all parts of our childhood versions.

I share this anecdote as a means of conveying how we set store by the values and traditions in our own histories. Indeed, this idea of a personal nostalgia is a strong force in forming our own identities. If asked what their favourite book is, or their favourite record or band, most people will think of something they read or heard when they were in their formative years: a book they read in sixth form, a band they saw at university. This emphasises the strong links between the concept of identity and belonging and the importance of history and our own personal history in developing understanding of the world and our place in it. Perhaps there is a sense of security in a book we first studied for A level or read as a teenager or, more deeply, perhaps we also consider the book we choose to be an aspect of who we are as a person and part of the person that we reveal of ourselves to the outside world.

Of course, our understanding of the world is initially formed by our immediate experiences, but soon we incorporate wider influences, which may include extended family but will also include influences and experiences that we encounter as we grow older. We make friends, we watch television, read books, develop interests, encounter other people (including teachers), use the internet, explore our local area and begin to form our own ideas. Understanding who we are and how we fit into the world is a central argument for the importance of history in the primary curriculum.

With each new influence we adapt, assimilate and change our views of the world, our influences and our perceptions. In a historical context, this will influence our thoughts and ideas about the world we live in based on our experiences of the past. With each continuing new influence, our perception of the past is further formed and the importance we place on the past is further defined.

Summary

This chapter has set out to identify what history is and why it is important. We have recognised that history is not only about the content (subject knowledge) but also about the process of history, as well as the many aspects of history that form our understanding of what history is actually all about. We have considered a wide and varied range of these aspects covering such things as chronology, change, interpretation, questioning, sequencing and identity. These aspects can be further organised into three distinct groups: historical skills, concepts, and attitudes and values. This helpful framework provides a key tool to support you as you plan and organiae your own lessons to provide a wide range of experiences for your pupils and enthuse them about history.

Finally, we have looked at the important place history holds in the curriculum and how history helps develop our understanding of the world, from our initial interactions with the world around us to the ever-increasing range of influences that come into our lives as we grow and develop. History as a subject can develop the whole child, including the ability to respect and tolerate differences, whether they be cultural, religious, societal or economic, and to appreciate the world in which we live.

Reflection point

Why is history important to you?

References

Cooper, H. (2012) *History 5–11. A Guide for Teachers*. Abingdon: Routledge.

Department for Education (2013) *The National Curriculum for England*. London: DfE.

Hoodless, P. (2008) *Teaching History in Primary Schools*. Exeter: Learning Matters.

Turner Bisset, R. (2005) *Creative Teaching: History in the Primary School*. London: Fulton.

2

History in the curriculum

This chapter approaches history in the curriculum from two angles: firstly, we explore the history of history in the curriculum; and secondly, we place that understanding in context alongside the language and rhetoric of the 2014 curriculum. In short, we address how the subject of history has been perceived in the past and how this has shaped its position in the primary curriculum today as well as the approaches we now take in delivering history in the curriculum.

The history of the history curriculum

Think back to your school days. There is a good chance that you can recall quite easily a trip to a museum or a visit to a historical site. You can probably remember a history project you completed or a class topic. You may well have gone to school dressed as a Tudor or a Victorian for a theme day based on your history topic that term. People tend to recall their history lessons fondly. Perhaps this is why there is so much debate surrounding the content of the history curriculum.

The past has always been important to every society, and indeed every stratum of society, and stories have traditionally been passed down orally. We know that this is how many Viking sagas were first relayed to the next generation. We also know that in some civilisations, such as the Sumerians and Greeks, writing became a way of recording their own histories. Awareness of audience is, similarly, of the upmost importance to those recording events, recognised as a means of shaping history by the stories left behind. We saw in Chapter 1 how history can be defined in different ways, such as local history, family history, popular history and personal histories. We also saw how representation of the past can be influenced and managed by those recording it. In primary school history, it is important that these features of history are not lost, even when teachers face a potentially difficult balance with the demands of delivering a curriculum that traditionally draws upon what we might refer to as the political history of the country. Hence, it is important that each practitioner is aware of what is considered good history practice and we need to remember to address the aspects of history that we identified in Chapter 1 in our history teaching. It is with this in mind that we can consider the evolution of the primary history curriculum.

The twentieth century provides the scene for one of the most fiercely fought battles in education: the place of history in the curriculum. The history of the history curriculum can be seen as a narrative of political leanings and thoughts on society as well as trends of the time. At the start of the last century, the history that was being taught in schools would mainly have consisted of stories of Britain's glorious past, with grand talk of empire, explorers and our great royal monarchs. History was very much the story of the 'great and the good' (Harnett, 2000). These were figures who could be held up as fine examples for our children to admire and aspire to. This can be very much seen as the rhetoric of the right. History was essentially British-centric, with qualities such as courage and loyalty at the forefront of many of the established stories. Harnett (2000) sheds light on the fact that, at this time, there was little distinction made in schools between a history lesson and a literature lesson. This lack of distinction between subjects goes some way to explain the 1959 reference to history as a subject 'for moral instruction' (Ministry of Education, 1959: 276), a statement that was made in response to a shift in the nature of history away from this 'glorious' narrative towards a more inquisitive subject. This perhaps provides the first indication that those governing schools and their curricula had an understanding of history's unique position as an instrument for social cohesion and control. It can be argued that successive rulers and governments have long recognised the importance of history as a governing mechanism for society.

A British-centric (or even Anglo-centric) history provided a comforting sense of well-being among the populace. For a long time, ideals of Britain's rightful place in the world, led by great statesmen, victorious in battle, as evidenced by the colour pink on proudly reproduced globes and maps of the time, sat well within education and those governing education. With these shared 'truths' seeming so appealing to all concerned and comforting for everyone, there was little reason for change. Children grew up assured that they had been born into the greatest nation on earth, while those governing were happy for this glorious narrative to be widely spread and taken to heart among the people. Nobody questioned what was being taught. As Slater (1989) and later Phillips (2000) point out, there was little need for government intervention. Even more recently, Davies and Redmond (2005) warn that there are still those who prefer this content style of history, when kings and queens and dates and facts were at the core of history lessons.

However, times change and what was once an accepted view of the world became challenged as Britain moved towards a more multicultural society, and views began similarly to change in terms of what should be taught. At the same time, history teaching itself began to alter. The narrative of British history, that long-standing view that history was a collection of stories about the great and the good, was changing. So, too, was the idea that lessons should mostly consist of learning dates and facts.

Phillips (2000) talks of a 'new history' that placed importance upon chronological understanding as well as conceptual understanding and skills. It should be noted, as Phillips does, that this was perhaps not 'new' at all and that Keatinge (1910) and Happold (1928) had previously considered such approaches in their thoughts on the delivery of history lessons, although such approaches were at the time firmly in the minority.

What were history lessons like in British primary schools in the 1960s, 1970s and 1980s? It is quite possible that you would not have had any history lessons at all, as history was optional until 1989 (Cooper, 2012). Perhaps as a result of the Plowden Report

(Central Advisory Council for Education, 1967), which advocated a more experiential approach towards the subject, many involved in primary education shied away from such approaches and history at the primary stage was left neglected in some quarters. This ties in with the view prevalent at the time that, within the context of child development, children cannot understand abstract concepts or hold any sense of understanding of the concept of time. The history that was taught in primary schools in the 1970s and 1980s was quite likely to have been taught in a cross-curricular or integrated manner. It was only in the last decades of the twentieth century that the curriculum introduced stand-alone statutory subjects, including history, which was identified as being about both content and process.

For example, my own history lessons as a pupil in primary school during the 1970s and early 1980s consisted of completing Ladybird History Work Cards. Each card comprised a Ladybird style illustration of the main protagonist or event opposite a couple of paragraphs of information. These sections of text were very much written in the 'great and the good' tradition. Overleaf, each card contained a comprehension activity entitled 'Do you remember?' These were to be neatly written out in your exercise book. Card 40, from the first set of Ladybird History Work Cards, focuses upon King Alfred and the Cakes (Figure 2.1). Through reading the text, we discover that King Alfred was 'not only wise, but was also kind and just'. This is representative of the image of Britain's history that was perpetuated through such resources.

As mentioned, it was not until the 1980s, and the curriculum changes later in that decade, that ideas of historical skills and concepts took a real hold and found a more secure footing in primary classrooms and in the curriculum itself. Much of the shift in ideas can be seen in the debates, reports and thoughts of the 1960s, 1970s and 1980s.

Figure 2.1 Ladybird History Work Cards

Ideas about how children learn had also been challenged, and this coincided now with a change in ideas as to what should be taught. Harnett (2000) tells us that Coltham and Fines (1971) supported the idea that history teaching should be defined by historical objectives, whilst the Schools Council History 13–16 Project (1976) believed that pupils should work as historians and undergo the same processes as 'real' historians, using similar sources of evidence. This built on ideas contained in the Hadow Report (Board of Education, 1931) which had suggested the use of historical sources such as pictures, museums and historical sites (Harnett, 2000).

This progressive approach to teaching history promotes ideas, such as historical skills and an understanding of the processes of history, that are a feature of what we would consider to be good practice today. Davies and Redmond (2005: 49) stress that primary history should 'plant the seeds of enquiry'. However, during the early 2000s, perhaps guided by *Excellence and Enjoyment* (Department for Education and Skills, 2003), schools began to move away from discrete subject teaching and to look for more creative and interesting ways to rethink the curriculum. In time, though, this led to a renewal of the old fears that the unique ideals of specific subjects, such as the aspects of history identified in Chapter 1, could easily get lost and that something needed to be done. The circle had completed one whole cycle and discussions began about a new curriculum.

So why is it important for us to know the history of the history curriculum? The answer is simple in that without an understanding of past history curricula it is impossible to know in which direction we are currently travelling (or whether we are going round in circles or not!). In the same way that a knowledge of our own past shapes our understanding and identity, a knowledge of our subject's past shapes our subject's future.

The curriculum

The Historical Association's (2011) Primary History Survey provided an interesting snapshot of history teaching across England at a most pertinent time. The survey found that, on average, over 1 hour a week was being spent on teaching history in our primary schools. Thirty-one per cent of teachers taught history as a discrete subject, which means that 69% still taught in a cross-curricular manner. Many schools stuck to the then prescribed history topics of the curriculum, and few ventured past the guidance provided by the Qualifications and Curriculum Development Agency, treating this a prescriptive rather than the non-statutory guidance it was intended to be (Jones, 2011). The survey provided some insight into the thoughts of teachers regarding the content of the curriculum and the fact that there was scope to investigate gender history, multicultural history and citizenship and diversity within the subject.

The *History for All* report of 2011 highlighted that children had a good knowledge of specific areas and that much history teaching in primary schools was good (Ofsted, 2011). However, it was this document that also highlighted the shortcomings in chronological understanding among children. This focus became a driving factor when it came to rewriting the history curriculum. This in turn led to a heated debate in the press, in schools and at Westminster as to what the new curriculum should look like. In much the same way as earlier debates questioned the content of what should be taught in schools, so too, this discussion re-questioned the content of the curriculum for the next generation. There was talk of 'our island story' having a prominent position in the curriculum – a return to the rhetoric of the past – and a 'traditional' content for the history curriculum. David Cameron, the British prime minister, when asked to pick his favourite childhood book selected the 1905 book *Our Island Story: A Child's History of England* by Henrietta Elizabeth Marshall, stating that 'it is written in a way that really captured my imagination and which nurtured my interest in the history of our great nation' (Hough, 2010).

Primary school history was defined from 1989 onwards, and the 1999 curriculum continued to lay out the intended historical ideals clearly, labelling sections as 'chronological understanding, knowledge and understanding of events, people and changes in the past, historical interpretation, historical enquiry and organisation and communication' (DfEE, 1999), as well as a breadth of study that covered the intended content for history lessons at Key Stages 1 and 2. Looking at this document, it could well be argued that chronology is not neglected here.

The word 'significant' is used to refer to people or events in the 1999 document, similarly a feature of the most recent curriculum. The word 'significant' is worthy of note as it not only appears in the 1999 document, but also in the consultation curriculum for primary history that was released in February 2013 (DfE, 2013a) and again in the final version, released in September 2013 (DfE, 2013b). Any curriculum proclaiming to study significant people could easily be associated with those figures, the great and the good, of twentieth-century history lessons that we looked at earlier. Hence, the curriculum proposed in the February 2013 document, was regarded as an insular one, speaking as it did of 'these islands', referring to Britain, and not including, for example, a study of the ancient Egyptians, a generally much-loved primary school staple.

Much was also made of the list-like narrative of the curriculum for Key Stage 2, which began with the Stone Age and ended with the 'glorious revolution'. As if to hammer home the point, chronology was described as 'essential'. The Historical Association (2013) formally responded, expressing the concern of various interest groups comprising professionals, practitioners and historians. There were, however, notable inclusions: for instance, historical concepts are highlighted, as are processes of historical enquiry, although these are not specifically named. School leaders, educators and concerned others, such as the Historical Association, warned of the dangers of such an inward-looking curriculum that harked back to the days of a British-centric outlook on the world, while museums and stately homes were concerned about visitor numbers should the Tudors, Victorians and ancient Egyptians disappear from the curriculum.

The final document, which appeared in September 2013, reinstated the Egyptians and provided more flexibility for primary schools to incorporate periods of history that fell beyond the 1066 cut-off point that heralded the end of the Key Stage 2 curriculum. The final document was less inward-looking, and the acknowledgement of the wider world featured more prominently than it had in the consultation document of seven months earlier.

As we can see from Table 2.1, the purpose of study appears more considered in the final version, although there are clear references to the processes of history in both versions. The inclusion of the phrase 'challenges of our time' and then later 'challenges of their time' is interesting. Is this a reference to social disquiet and unrest? A reference

Table 2.1 Comparison of purpose of study

	Purpose of Study
February 2013	A high-quality history education equips pupils to think critically, weigh evidence, sift arguments, and develop perspective and judgement. A knowledge of Britain's past, and our place in the world, helps us understand the challenges of our own time.
September 2013	A high-quality history education will help pupils gain a coherent knowledge and understanding of Britain's past and that of the wider world. It should inspire pupils' curiosity to know more about the past. Teaching should equip pupils to ask perceptive questions, think critically, weigh evidence, sift arguments, and develop perspective and judgement. History helps pupils to understand the complexity of people's lives, the process of change, the diversity of societies and relationships between different groups, as well as their own identity and the challenges of their time.

to multicultural Britain? Was this written in the light of the 2011 summer riots? Is this an echo, in the 2014 curriculum, of former history curricula that once were used as tools for social cohesion?

While the final document is less list-like, it still promotes the chronological element of Britain's history that will see the children continue to study post-1066 eras at Key Stage 3. However, teachers and history coordinators have more freedom to present some topics that fall beyond 1066 at Key Stage 2. This is because a local history study unit and a chronological study unit that focuses on an aspect or theme that goes beyond 1066 have been included in the 2014 curriculum. This is particularly welcome as it provides an opportunity for teachers to look at familiar topics, such as the Tudors, the Victorians or the Second World War, in a new and interesting way. We will look at planning for this in a later chapter.

Although there is no legal requirement to teach the 2014 curriculum in a chronological order, there can be no denying that the desire to improve chronological understanding is a driving factor of the latest national curriculum for history. The *History for All* report has thus had a major influence upon the content and structure of the history curriculum for Key Stages 2 and 3.

Michael Maddison, formerly of Ofsted where he was national lead for history, wrote an article for the Historical Association's *Primary History* in the spring of 2014. At that time he saw history teaching as a subject in transition, noting that pupils' 'knowledge and understanding of the topics studied' had declined since the time of *History for All*, adding that history teaching had become 'more variable' and that when it was poor, there was no way of 'ensuring that the aims of the history curriculum [had] been fulfilled'. As with the *History for All* report, it was noted that chronological understanding was not good among pupils. Several reasons were cited for this, including the episodic nature of the then history curriculum, the non-chronological teaching of units, the lack of links made between history topics and the lack of timelines in classroom displays.

Tellingly, Maddison makes the point that the best pupil knowledge and evidence of progression occurred in schools where history was taught as a discrete subject, stating that the 'growing popularity of a topic or thematic curriculum . . . has increasingly undermined the identity and integrity of history'. The importance of 'subject-specific aims' is reiterated: 'Too often history is submerged within an integrated curriculum and, as a result, pupils' knowledge and understanding has suffered.'

Maddison moves on to herald enquiry as the most beneficial approach to teaching history, stating that in successful schools 'a culture of resourcefulness, investigation and problem-solving' was evident, which developed pupils' ability in research, analysis, evaluation and communication in their later studies. The final observation of the state of history teaching at the dawn of the 2014 curriculum was that history teaching was best when it 'develops pupils' historical knowledge and historical thinking'. With this in mind, Maddison emphasises the importance of the purpose of study of the 2014 curriculum as well as the aims that are set out within the document.

With this in mind, you are encouraged to create units that provide overviews of some subject areas as well as more in-depth studies of other areas, the choice of which may well depend upon the location of your school. For instance, a school in Chester is unlikely to take an overview approach to a topic on the Romans.

Looking specifically at Key Stage 1, Russell (2015) agrees with Maddison in that there is little change between the requirements for history at Key Stage 1 within the current curriculum document and the previous curriculum. This allows many practitioners to build upon their plans and provide purposeful and meaningful lessons. However, a potential barrier here, as Maddison highlights, is a lack of subject knowledge. This is not a new concern. The Primary History Survey (Historical Association, 2011) highlighted that teachers themselves were keen to develop their own subject knowledge through continued professional development (CPD) and were keen to explore ways of doing this. Table 2.2 sets out Maddison's views as to what makes good and outstanding teaching and learning experiences in primary history.

Adapted from Maddison (2014)

The 2014 curriculum, however, does not address how to teach chronology (or history in general, for that matter), only that it should be taught. Davies and Redmond (2005) suggest that teaching in chronological order consolidates an understanding of chronology within the minds of children. Schools that I work with have addressed this matter in different ways. Some schools have always adopted a chronological structure for their long-term plans and have done so from a time that pre-dates the current curriculum.

Table 2.2 Good and outstanding history

Good and outstanding history comes when...	– history is taught as a discrete subject – teachers focus on a structured enquiry – teaching develops historical knowledge and historical thinking – children can demonstrate their historical understanding

Other schools have chosen topics and eras that they feel best suit the needs of their children in line with the opportunities, experiences and expertise within their staff that they can offer.

Plotting the 2014 curriculum for Key Stage 2 might produce something like the map in Table 2.3. I first presented this table in Russell (2015) along with a rationale for placing each unit as above. This was primarily to keep a chronological focus for the British history units. The other units have been placed where they could have the most impact upon pupils and their developing historical understanding. Other considerations in the table include the SATs in May, whilst the gaps indicate time when topics could be expanded or schools could choose to include an entirely new topic of their own selection. It should be remembered that the national curriculum is a minimum requirement and that schools can add to the units as they see fit. Schools with split classes will, of course, be adept at creating a two-year rotation in order to provide full coverage for their learners.

This is by no means a definitive mapping document for Key Stage 2. It is not meant to be, rather merely the start of a dialogue in trying to achieve an interesting curriculum while maintaining an element of chronological understanding.

So far, our thoughts regarding the 2014 curriculum have focused upon the impact at Key Stage 2. Russell (2015) highlighted the changes at Key Stage 1, arguing that there is little change at all between the 2000 national curriculum and the 2014 curriculum. The School History Project (SHP) made the same point at its inaugural Primary History Conference at the British Museum in March 2014. In the same way that changes at Key Stage 2 can be interpreted by practitioners in new and exciting ways, the Key Stage 1 curriculum offers similar opportunities.

Perhaps most intriguing is a focus on pairings of significant people such as Christopher Columbus and Neil Armstrong, comparing aspects of life in different periods and the impact these people had on the world around them. Russell (2015) highlights that the 'significant lives' for study are non-statutory. This means that the chosen lives for study are primarily at the discretion of each individual school. Similarly, schools delivering the Key Stage 1 curriculum are required to study an event that goes beyond living memory. The curriculum itself suggests the Great Fire of London or the

Table 2.3 The Mapping Table KS2

| | Key Stage 2 History Curriculum Map | | |
	Autumn	Spring	Summer
Year 3	Achievements of earliest civilisations	Ancient Greece	Changes in Britain from the Stone Age to Iron Age
Year 4	The Roman Empire and its impact on Britain		Britain's settlement by Anglo-Saxons and Scots
Year 5	The Viking and Anglo-Saxon struggle for the Kingdom of England	Local history study	Study of an aspect or theme
Year 6	A non-European society		

Table 2.4 Mapping Table for Key Stage 1

	Key Stage 1 History Curriculum Map		
	Autumn	*Spring*	*Summer*
Year 1	Changes within living memory		Significant historical events, people and places in their own locality
Year 2	Events beyond living memory		Lives of significant individuals

first aeroplane flight or events that are commemorated through festivals or anniversaries, and of course many schools are likely to follow this guidance, although the final decision rests with the school.

A mapping document for Key Stage 1 might look something like Table 2.4. Again I would note that the gaps in the spring term for both Years 1 and 2 provide some flexibility. You could use that time to develop schemes of work, or, as is the case with the lives of significant individuals, perhaps take the opportunity to study other people. Events beyond living memory are included in the autumn term, but once again the opportunity to study more than one event could be accommodated within the blank spaces. Again, this is not included here as a definitive mapping document for Key Stage 1, but simply as a visual reference for how the Key Stage 1 curriculum could be mapped out.

Turner Bisset (2005) highlights how understanding the nature of the history curriculum helps to inform the teaching approaches and planning of the delivery of activities that we, as teachers, create for our children. This is something that we will investigate throughout the rest of the book.

Summary

In this chapter we have explored the history of the history curriculum, discovering that the rhetoric of the right was prevalent through much of the nineteenth and twentieth centuries and that such thinking is still evident in our curriculum today. We have also explored how thinking in teaching and the way in which children learn has had an impact upon ideas about what children should learn in their history lessons and how they should learn it. From here, we looked at the debates that led to the current curriculum and its focus on a content and processes approach regarding what history should be taught. We have also considered how a school may address long-term plans in order to accommodate the topics highlighted in the 2014 curriculum.

References

Board of Education (1931) *Report of the Consultative Committee on the Primary School.* London: HMSO.

Central Advisory Council for Education (1967) *Children and Their Primary Schools* (Plowden Report). London: HMSO.

Coltham, J. and Fines, J. (1971) *Educational Objectives for the Study of History*. London: Historical Association.

Cooper, H. (2012) *History 5–11: A Guide for Teachers*. Abingdon: Routledge.

Davies, J. and Redmond, J. (2005) *Coordinating History across the Primary School*. London: Fulton.

Department for Education (2013a) *The National Curriculum for England: Framework Document for Consultation*. London: DfE.

Department for Education (2013b) *The National Curriculum for England*. London: DfE.

Department for Education and Employment (1999) *The National Curriculum: Handbook for Primary Teachers in England*. London: DfEE.

Department for Education and Skills (2003) *Excellence and Enjoyment: A Strategy for Primary Schools*. London: DfES.

Happold, F.C. (1928) *The Approach to History*. London: Christophers.

Harnett, P. (2000) Curriculum decision-making in the primary school: The place of history. In J. Arthur and R. Phillips (eds), *Issues in History Teaching*. London: Routledge.

Historical Association (2011) Primary History Survey (England): History 3–11. http://www.history.org.uk/resources/primary_resource_8636.html (accessed 26 February 2016).

Historical Association (2013) HA response to the National Curriculum consultation April 2013. http://www.history.org.uk/news/news_1779.html (accessed 19 January 2016).

Hough, A. (2010) Revealed: David Cameron's favourite childhood book is Our Island Story. *Daily Telegraph*, 29 October. http://www.telegraph.co.uk/culture/books/booknews/8094333/Revealed-David-Camerons-favourite-childhood-book-is-Our-Island-Story.html (accessed 26 February 2016).

Jones, M. (2011) What history should we teach? The teachers' perspective: The Historical Association's Primary Survey. *Primary History* 57.

Keatinge, M. (1910) *Studies in the Teaching of History*. London: Black.

Maddison, M. (2014) The National Curriculum for History from September 2014: The view from Ofsted. *Primary History* 66.

Ministry of Education (1959) *Primary Education. Suggestions for the Consideration of Teachers and Others Concerned with the Work of Primary Schools*. London: HMSO.

Ofsted (2011) *History for All*. Manchester: Ofsted.

Phillips, R. (2000) Government policies, the state and the teaching of history. In J. Arthur and R. Phillips (eds), *Issues in History Teaching*. London: Routledge.

Russell, C. (2015) History. In M. Webster and S. Misra (eds), *Teaching the Primary Foundation Subjects*. Maidenhead: Open University Press.

Schools Council History 13–16 Project (1976) *A New Look at History*. Edinburgh: Holmes McDougall.

Slater, J. (1989) *The Politics of History Teaching: A Humanity Dehumanised?* London: University of London Institute of Educxation.

Turner Bisset, R. (2005) *Creative Teaching: History in the Primary School*. London: Fulton.

3

Teaching history

This chapter explores our new understanding of what history is and begins to investigate the ways in which we may approach teaching history in the primary school. The chapter considers the best methods for teaching history, including an appraisal of cross-curricular approaches, opportunities for developing thinking skills, an exploration of holistic approaches as well as enquiry.

History is often cited by teachers as one of their favourite subjects to teach, irrespective of their own subject background. The Primary History Survey found that children and teachers alike enjoyed history (Historical Association, 2011). This may well be because history is often seen as an umbrella subject (Cooper, 2012) that covers many facets of primary school life. Certainly it is not hard to draw subjects together through history: think of mosaics and art, or pyramids and DT, for example. Similarly, we could design mathematical word problems based upon the history units we have been studying. Of course, we might be straying from Maddison's (2014) view of discrete subject teaching here, but more of that later.

Davies and Redmond (2005) identify two main aims of school history: firstly, to develop a sense of identity through learning about Britain, Europe and the wider world; and secondly, to introduce pupils to 'what is involved in understanding and interpreting the past' (p. 49). These aims are as relevant today as ever they were. The second point clearly identifies the processes of history as being just as important as the content of history, and we should keep this in mind as we design, plan and deliver our history lessons and schemes of work.

Our history lessons need to maintain a purposeful and meaningful historical set of objectives, with success criteria and assessment outcomes rooted in historical goals. Alongside this, history teaching needs to take into account our understanding and developing philosophy of what history is, by which I mean what 'good history teaching' is.

As we have seen, history teaching for a long time was influenced by the political ideals of the time and by how it was thought children accommodated information and learned. Much of this thinking was influenced by the work of Piaget (1936) who set out the stages of child development by age, implying that children were beginning to accommodate logical thought processes between the ages of 7 and 11½ and that it was only at the age of 11½ that children could think in abstract and logical ways. Given that

Hoodless (2008: 3) describes history as 'the most abstract subject in the curriculum' and that the history curriculum has for some time considered concepts such as change and continuity, chronology and evidence, this has had an impact upon the way in which we think of history teaching today. Cooper (2012) indicates that children can work at any level if the work is presented in a suitable and achievable manner. It is, therefore, accepted that children can achieve high levels of historical understanding as well as knowledge, as evidenced by Ofsted (2011) and Maddison (2014).

Of course, there are many ways of approaching teaching history and much of these are driven by our interpretation of what history is. Dean and the Nuffield Primary History Project (2011) see history as 'a process of enquiry' and 'an evidence-based interpretation' of the past. This, as we have seen, is clearly indicated in the curriculum and will have a big impact on the appropriate types of activities and lessons for children to engage with.

Maddison, as we noted in Chapter 2, referred to one particular approach to teaching history: a discrete subject approach. However, you are likely to be familiar with the phrase 'cross-curricular approach', which can mean different things to different people. Add in 'thematic teaching' to the mix and 'integrated curriculum' for good measure and it is more than possible to be at cross-purposes. To my mind, a cross-curricular approach combines two or more curriculum subjects in one lesson. Therefore, a lesson that investigated sources relating to the reputation of Sir Francis Drake but also included the children creating 'Wanted' posters or writing biographies (depending upon their findings) would be a cross-curricular one.

A 'thematic approach' is somewhat different. Lesson plans are at times shaped by a topic approach. For instance, 'tea' might be the topic or theme for an entire term's work across all curriculum subjects. In this way, geography lessons might look at areas of the world where tea is grown, science lessons may investigate the efficiency of a range of teacups in keeping the tea warm, and history lessons would explore the Empire, tea trade routes, customs and the all-round history of tea. In this way, such an approach might be considered more as an 'integrated curriculum', where links have been made to one specific starting point (in this case tea). There is of course still the possibility here of lessons being taught as discrete subjects with only the theme as a link between disciplines.

As we have seen, Maddison (2014) and Ofsted (2011) advocate a discrete approach and the curriculum itself is presented as discrete subjects, so why is there a discussion about teaching approaches at all? Such debate arises when the uniqueness of the subject is perceived to be at risk. The *History for All* report hints at a mistrust of cross-curricular based lessons, yet we note that in the Primary History Survey (Historical Association, 2011) 69% of teachers described their teaching as cross-curricular. Cooper (2012) recognises the benefits of cross-curricular teaching, but there is a cautionary tone here and Cooper also highlights the findings of the report, adding that 'where teaching was cross-curricular, planning for progression in developing historical knowledge was limited and that pupils' perceptions of history were sometimes unclear' (p. 5). She goes on to say that the 'integrity of the subject' remains intact as long as the historical elements of the lesson are clearly defined. So there seems to be an imbalance between teaching in school and the preferred methods advocated by interested bodies.

Over the years there has been much debate as to the best method to teach history. The Plowden Report (Central Advisory Council for Education, 1967) stated that the separation of the curriculum into individual subjects was detrimental to children's thinking and engagement. This view is shaped by the idea that life is not experienced in neat compartmentalised sections and that the intricacies of history were not suitable for children. Running alongside these ideas was the thought, as we have seen, that conceptual understanding was beyond the capabilities of young children.

More recent arguments have focused upon the idea that children of any age can handle difficult concepts. We already know that the curriculum has, since the 1990s, included reference to historical skills and concepts as well as historical content, and so we need to think about how we can structure learning experiences effectively in order to cover all the aspects of history that we identified in Chapter 1. Davies and Redmond (2005) propose that in order to develop children's historical thinking the teacher needs to provide opportunities for the children to engage with questioning. This would appear to be a sensible suggestion, but it emphasises the shift in thinking about what a history lesson should look like. In 1998, when this was originally written, this would have been a far cry from what many activities posing as history lessons would have looked like. Many would have been far more akin to comprehension exercises. So we are now thinking of the individual strands of history and how these would sit together to create a lesson or a series of lessons.

We saw in Chapter 1 that history comprises enquiry, chronological understanding, interpretation, evidence, empathy and concepts such as change, continuity and different points of view. Such a focused approach towards the teaching of history ensures that old accusations of history teaching being 'vague, woolly and fragmented' (Pickford *et al.* 2013: 152) are laid to one side. History lessons need to avoid low-level engagement and the dreaded three Cs (cutting, copying and colouring). As Mortimore *et al.* and Alexander *et al.* (cited in Turner Bisset, 2005: 16) point out, such activities lead to 'less effective teaching'.

From our reading so far, it is clear that many organisations and educationalists place much more importance on a hands-on enquiry approach to teaching history (Cooper, 2012; Pickford *et al.*, 2013). This is seen as the best method of teaching history and helping children understand the past. Enquiry suggests an investigation, a lesson in which the children will be engaged with artefacts and pieces of evidence and asked to put together the pieces in order to create a picture of the past – like some sort of time-travelling three-dimensional jigsaw puzzle. In my experience, children love this kind of lesson and respond well to investigations involving real source materials. To them, it somehow does not feel like a lesson, not even like learning, but 'doing history' in this way is arguably the most valuable way of engaging in the past.

As a history teacher, you will be accustomed to saving odd items that you think will sooner or later 'come in handy' in the classroom. Old stamps, booklets, flyers, maps, newspapers, adverts, film posters and commemorative mugs – in fact, just about anything – can become artefacts and get added to your resource bank.

Over the years, I've amassed a number of artefacts that I use as part of a 'suitcase activity' (Figure 3.1). I'm not entirely sure who first thought of this practical lesson idea, but I've come across it in various guises over many years. Essentially, you collect together items from a particular era, perhaps from the roaring twenties, the rock 'n' roll fifties or the Second World War. The children, through exploring each artefact, are encouraged to make judgements, interpret evidence and pose questions. In doing so

Figure 3.1 The suitcase activity

they are taking part in historical enquiry and developing their historical skills. (More on this later in Chapter 4.)

In comparison with less practical lessons, engaging children with artefacts and challenging them to ask questions about the past is a stimulating learning experience. It is worthwhile and purposeful in helping the children achieve the requirements of the curriculum and appreciate life in times gone by. Sources can include any number of items from written documents to maps, photographs, street names, buildings and television programmes. This rich range of sources is both engaging and inspiring, giving history, and the study of history, a wide appeal. When we talk about the processes of finding out about the past, we find that enquiry is at the beating heart of good history teaching.

Some schools set a question as the driving force for a whole topic or lesson. For example, at the time of writing, the question 'would you rather be a gladiator or a premiership footballer?' is a popular enquiry in Year 4 classes. Such a title provides a line of enquiry with the rich sources of evidence open for teachers to select and develop as they see fit to suit the individual needs of their class. Through this enquiry, the children will no doubt draw their own conclusions and will be encouraged to present their findings in all manner of ways. In doing so, the children are actively engaged in an investigation, they are adopting the persona of a historian or a detective. They are examining themes, topics and artefacts. They are developing the ability to 'ask perceptive questions, think critically, weigh evidence and sift arguments' (DfE, 2013). By posing questions the children can develop their historical skills and progress through several of the stages in their bid to investigate their given area.

A large part of the investigation, or enquiry, is piecing together the evidence to make sense of what has been discovered. Reflecting upon what our enquiry has told us about the past and interpreting our findings must be part of the process of history for our children too. This provides us with a deeper understanding of the past overall. This stage in the development of children's knowledge and understanding is essential in providing a fully rounded and coherent understanding of the past.

Cooper (2012) highlights a concern raised by Ofsted (2011), Alexander (2010) and by teachers through the Historical Association (2011), that teachers themselves do not have a confident or secure understanding of what is involved in a historical enquiry. This, in turn, as Cooper (2012) explains, has an impact on the types of activities that are set, the objectives for the enquiry and the quality of the assessment (both formative and summative) that takes place. In terms of progression, a lack of understanding has a detrimental impact upon the ability of the teacher to plan for progression in terms of the thinking skills that are to be developed. So enquiry is more than simply asking questions. Enquiry is making sense of what has been uncovered and consideration of factors such as the sources used and the interpretation of the findings.

When considering historical sources, these are split into two groups: primary and secondary. Primary sources are artefacts that are of the time. In other words, they were around when the person lived or the event occurred: for example, an old letter, a newspaper or a china vase. Secondary sources are created after the event, such as a documentary or a book published today about the Second World War. Understanding these distinctions is the first step towards interrogating source materials, checking the validity of the source and the provenance of a piece. In addition, considering potential bias and questioning why something was produced, who produced it and to what effect, is part and parcel of using source materials. Another consideration is the nature of the source. Does an artefact tell the whole story or one aspect of the story? If an archaeologist, years from now, were to find a gold cup in my back garden, does that mean that we all sat around in 2016 drinking from gold cups or does it just happen to be one gold cup that was lost? (Incidentally, as far as I know, there are no gold cups in my back garden.) This might tell us something about the level of society we are looking at, whether this was a rich area or a poor part of town. We might place male/female interpretations on the source. Without context, our source may provide us with little information. We need to consider the attitudes and values as highlighted in Chapter 1, and that, at times, we might not know everything there is to know. At best, we might be able to provide a 'best fit' educated guess.

At times, it can be good to present 'mystery items' from the past, only to reveal their true purpose after some wild guessing. This is clearly 'inspiring curiosity' (DfE, 2013). Sources can also prompt other aspects of history, such as historical imagination. For instance, as mentioned earlier, in seminars I use an old suitcase that contains several items from 1942 (Figure 3.1). One of the items is a box of dominoes. Each domino is smooth and particularly tactile. It is easy, with these in your hand, to wonder about who might have played with these dominoes in the past. Given the links to the Second World War, and the other items in the case alluding to the owner being a pilot, it is also easy to imagine what that person might have been facing and how he would have been feeling. As a note of caution, there are dangers with this kind of historical imagination as we might go too far in our fanciful thoughts, we might romanticise the situation and lose sight of the evidence and the likelihood of the reality that the evidence is really suggesting.

Sometimes our reasoning is born of our interpretation of sources and historical imagination and, as we have already identified, this might be a 'best fit' or educated guess based upon the most likely set of events. We will never know if the dominoes were

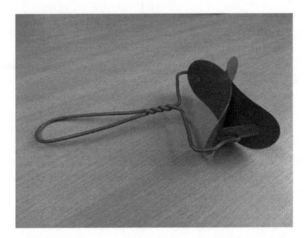

Figure 3.2 Mystery object

used to pass time before the pilot was scrambled to fend off the Luftwaffe or not. We can only imagine. We can only infer and more importantly, we can engage the children in the processes of history within their lessons.

In other cases, coming to conclusions might be a lot more straightforward. We might know exactly when an artefact was used and who used it. Figure 3.2 shows a household object that dates back to the late Victorian period. Although modern-day equivalents exist that look almost identical, we can use artefacts such as this in order to 'inspire pupils' curiosity to know more about the past' (DfE, 2013). We could challenge the children to identify the room in the house where the item might have been used, and what it would be used for. Using artefacts as mystery objects like this enables you to prompt questions from the children and to hone their enquiry skills. The children could play a 'yes/no' game in order to find out more about the object. Once the children have uncovered what the object is, they can investigate the era in more detail and the lives of the people that would have used the artefact. In this way, the children add to their knowledge and understanding of the period. In case you are unsure as to what this object is, the answer is at the end of this chapter.

We have already begun to explore interpretations of sources. Cooper (2012) highlights that interpretations of the past concern themselves with changes in time and changes in place. We should also remind ourselves of the concept of historiography here, for even in selecting the sources to be used in a lesson, the teacher is colouring the potential outcomes and findings and making judgements as to what is and what is not worthy of note in the lesson. Culturally, too, our interpretation of events and artefacts will alter through time and place.

Understanding accounts of the past is also important. It may seem daunting to face such a concept in the primary school, but think of the success of the *Horrible Histories* books and television series. This is a clear indication that children can cope with different types of interpretations of the past.

Although perhaps less known now, a similar example is offered by some of the *Carry On* films that depicted life in times gone by, *Carry On Cleo* and *Carry On Henry* being good examples of interpretations of history. More recently, *Blackadder* was criticised by the then secretary of state for education for trivialising history, when it could be argued that this is not the case at all.

As we identified earlier, 'good' use of accounts and interpretations of the past can help address many of the attributes of history that are set out in the purpose of study in the curriculum. There is a need to be aware of not only our own interpretations of evidence, but also the interpretations that have been put in place before. Therefore, teaching history well is a fine balance between not only enquiry, but also consideration of the sources and interpretation, and enquiry is only one approach to use in our history lessons.

Heritage education is increasing in importance in providing meaningful learning experiences. I am currently conducting research into the effectiveness and impact of visits to historical sites. This builds on the findings of Wollins *et al.* (1992) and Falk and Dierking (1997), who have looked at school visits as part of an education programme.

Hickmott and Chiasson (2014) claim that 'site visits are good for children', and this would seem to be an accepted truth. Certainly the access to experts in the field is an attraction for many teachers and offsets the challenges of organising such trips. The benefits of a school visit to a historic site should stem from the fact that the children can engage with activities, see things and experience things that they could not otherwise do in school.

The primary history curriculum may not refer specifically to school trips, but it does suggest the study of a 'site' in the local history unit at Key Stage 2 as well as referring to a 'range of sources' that are to be used in investigating the past. A well-structured and focused trip will help you address aspects of the purpose of study and the aims of the curriculum. You should not organise a trip simply because you happen to be a school near a priory or a Roman amphitheatre; it should be driven by a specific set of requirements and learning objectives that are best met through such a visit. Similarly, as a teacher, you will want to assess the effectiveness of the trip in order to measure progression and assess the children's understanding.

A school trip to a museum, gallery or historical site will, in many cases, form part of a topic from the curriculum. As such, most sites will have prepared materials and education officers. The National Trust, at some properties and sites, provides fantastic supporting materials for group visits. At certain properties, teachers are offered the opportunity to run a 'self-led' visit using materials that are available through the education team and online.[1] Similarly, Historic England says that 'we want every child to be inspired by their local heritage'.[2] The Heritage Schools programme, set up in response to the government's report on cultural education, aims 'to help children develop a sense of pride in where they live, to understand their local heritage and how it relates to the national story' and 'to help teachers be more confident in making effective use of local heritage resources in delivering the curriculum'.[2] These aims would seem applicable to good history teaching, and therefore we can see that such a government-funded programme instils a sense of importance in heritage education in teaching the primary curriculum.

---

[1]http://www.nationaltrust.org.uk
[2]http://www.historicengland.org.uk

Hickmott and Chiasson (2014) give further credence to the use of historic sites. They state that children require expert 'knowledge as an important building block for thinking'. They also point out that using a local heritage site helps 'ground children in their own locality'. It caters for different learning styles and levels of enthusiasm. Children can benefit from a change in the norm, and being outside and with other adults might make the experience more memorable.

The structure and focus of the visit needs to be in place for the visit to be meaningful. A clear intent for the visit needs to be shared between the teacher and the education officers at the site. The use of support materials needs to be carefully considered, too. While these resources can be a great source of information and ideas, they have often not been written with a specific age range in mind, they may not have been designed to cater for the specific needs of the children in individual classes, so they will need to be adapted to be as effective as you would want them to be.

Museum trips and visits to galleries and other historic sites embrace the ideals set out in the *Learning Outside the Classroom Manifesto* (Department for Education and Skills, 2006). The Council for Learning Outside the Classroom state that 'every young person (0–19yrs) should experience the world beyond the classroom as an essential part of learning and personal development'.[3] The Council highlights that learning outside can take place just about anywhere, listing heritage sites, farms, the built environment as well as school grounds, adventure settings and sacred spaces. Among the perceived benefits of learning outside the classroom are improved 'academic achievement', higher-order learning, developing 'skills and independence' and improved 'attitudes to learning' as well as a reduction in 'behavioural problems'.

Dean (2013) states that the benefits of learning outside the classroom for primary history are that 'children can investigate, observe, wonder, record and create historical knowledge and understand their world'. I would suggest, too, that learning outside the classroom is a uniquely memorable occasion, making learning fun and exciting. The fact that it can include the school grounds, a history walk in the neighbourhood as well as a trip to a ruin or a coastline means that children gain different benefits at different times. Outside experiences can be revisited, enabling understanding of the past to be consolidated and built upon with each subsequent experience.

Children can investigate questions such as 'how has my street changed?' This could combine sources such as letters, maps and photographs with observations made whilst exploring their street. Casting the net wider, children could investigate change over time in a specific area, for instance, the trade in a particular area, tourism or ecological concerns arising from the increase in numbers of tourists in places such as the Lake District, Brecon Beacons or Snowdonia.

This could be a good opportunity to combine two teaching approaches and challenge the children with an enquiry while using the outdoors as a resource bank. In the case of the local area, this could include date stones, street names, pub signs and emblems on street furniture. These all become artefacts. Couple this with a trip to the local records office or public library and the children are engaged in a data-rich environment that calls upon all their new-found skills in order to piece together a picture of the past in their home town.

---

[3]http://www.lotc.org.uk/

Objects have always been an essential part of history investigations, whether it be a Stone Age bone needle or an ancient amulet. In recent years, objects have been the focus of much of our historical awareness. The fantastic joint venture between the British Museum and the BBC, *The History of the World in 100 Objects* (2010), was not only an enjoyable radio programme but also an interactive website, a book (McGregor, 2010) and a podcast. This spawned several similarly inspired books, such as *A History of Cricket in 100 Objects* (Mortimer, 2013) and *A History of Football in 100 Objects* (Mortimer, 2012). A rich vein for other interpretations too, this idea of examining an object can be seen as essential to our history teaching.

The BBC–British Museum project sets out to explore history in a new way. Indeed, the director of the project stated that 'by focusing on things rather than just dates, eras and regions, you realize that the history we were taught at school was simply not adequate any more if we are properly to understand the world in which we live' (McGregor, cited in BBC and British Museum, 2013). You may or may not agree with the sentiment here, but certainly we can agree that there is a lot to be gained by exploring artefacts in terms of what the item was made for, how it was made, looked after and preserved. Interestingly, items included in the project told of the many aspects of life in the past, such as political, economic and cultural. This is a clear link back to our understanding of what good primary history is in terms of the aspects of history we explored in Chapter 1.

Of course, teachers and schools can use the objects from the series by accessing the book, podcasts and website. However, others will see this as an opportunity to produce their own version of the project within their school. Indeed, the children themselves could choose the artefacts. The project itself included hundreds of suggestions from 'over 350 museum venues across the UK'. Not all made it to the final 100 but these additional objects 'were uploaded to the website and are available to view in each individual venue' (British Museum and BBC, 2013). Of course, the project itself was not created specifically to teach history to primary school children; however, at the time of the project, there was a spin-off CBBC programme called *Relic: Guardians of the Museum* that encouraged children to become detectives. This included exploring the Easter Island statue and the Rosetta Stone among other objects in the British Museum collection (British Museum and BBC, 2013). In addition to this, BBC Learning produced lesson plans for primary schools that explored the objects that featured in the CBBC programme. This aspect of the project also included opportunities to explore objects from a more local perspective.

This project serves as inspiration for you and for history coordinators to develop their own museum of artefacts. This could be an eclectic mix of items or a museum with a specific theme, such as 'toys' or 'the Second World War'. At my university, I have created, on a small scale, a museum that showcases items from different eras. The trainee teachers I work with are challenged to provide information cards and suitable activities for each of the items. These are to be shared through QR codes straight to the trainee, where they can tweak and adapt resources and add further ideas to the bank of resources they have collectively created.

The use of artefacts is an essential part of being a historian. Interpreting an object to provide focus on an aspect of the past is a valuable historical skill.

The teaching of history in the primary school is well placed to address the development of thinking skills among our children. Thinking skills themselves have long been part of the debate as to what should be taught at school and the ability to 'be thought-ful', to analyse and to respond effectively and in a considered manner are attributes most would want to develop in our children.

At the turn of the century, McGuinness (1999), building upon the work of Feuerstein (1980), Lipman *et al.* (1980) and De Bono (1992), raised awareness of the need for think-ing skills to be developed in the classroom. McGuinness's paper was essentially a review of the current practice and led to thinking skills being adopted more purposefully in schools. It highlighted that thinking skills in lessons were most evident in history and geography lessons, indicating that practitioners had long recognised the strong opportunities that were presented through history in enabling their pupils to think and respond to the materials, evidence and stories of the past.

McGuinness's paper led to a range of books becoming available, including Belle Wallace's respected *Using History to Develop Thinking Skills at Key Stage 2* (2003). A quick search on the internet will reveal a whole host of similarly related texts on the promotion of thinking skills in the classroom, indicating that this is still an area of inter-est and common concern.

One of the best at devising practical activities is the late Paul Ginnis and his acclaimed *Teacher's Toolkit* (2002). I was lucky enough to attend a CPD course run by Paul during my teaching days. It was an affirming experience, as his beliefs about education were in close accord with my own in an education world that often seems splintered and disillusioned with itself. On that day, Paul implemented several activities that utilised history curriculum content but were designed to develop thinking skills and independence. One example consisted of real historical scenarios that had been faced by people of the past, for instance, a king in battle with a tactical decision to make. Along with the scenario there was a selection of responses, one of which was the actual decision that the king had taken at the time. The task was for the pupils to discuss each of the responses and to reason and rationalise which one they thought was true. At this stage, children will toy with ideas and provide justification for the actions in the provided responses. The teacher can control the session by structuring the activity in different ways, Dialogic talk could be promoted here, additional information could be introduced or one of the responses could be removed from the frame. Step by step the children come to realise the true response to the scenario. The actual response may be surprising, especially when placing our twenty-first-century sensibilities upon the peo-ple of the past. As we discovered in Chapter 1, our interpretations of 'normal behaviour' apply to our experiences of the world we live in and those interpretations of 'normal' will alter over time.

Hoodless (2008) identifies thinking skills relating to history as information process-ing, reasoning, enquiry, creative thinking and evaluation, stating that these skills 'con-tribute to problem solving' (p. 42).

Much has been made of Bloom's taxonomy (Bloom *et al.* 1956) and Anderson and Krathwohl's (2000) adaptation with the stages of the taxonomy being labelled as either lower-order thinking skills or higher-order thinking skills. A model such as Bloom's tax-onomy can act as a useful tool for planning, especially when taking on board cue words that can direct activities and discussions in the classroom (Table 3.1).

Cooper (2012: 146) identifies that the Cambridge Review (Alexander, 2010) high-lighted that 'an overcrowded primary curriculum had eliminated opportunities for

Table 3.1 Table of Bloom's attributes, cue words and questions

Stage	Attributes	Cue Words	Questions
Knowledge	Recalling facts	Who, what, why, when, find, list, recall	How? What? Can? Did?
Comprehension	Demonstrating understanding	Compare, explain, interpret	Can you explain...?
Application	Solving problems using new information	Apply, choose, organise, sequence	How would you use...? How would you solve...?
Analysis	Making inferences	Analyse, categorise	What are the features of...?
Synthesis	Assimilating information	Formulate ideas, build knowledge	What is the impact...?
Evaluation	Presenting new knowledge	Conclude, justify, dispute	What are your thoughts...?

activities that involved thought, talk, problem solving and meaningful and rewarding in-depth studies across the curriculum'. This itself is addressed by Cooper, but it again serves as a reminder of the tight timetabling within which schools operate and the rigours and challenges teachers face as well as the demands of SATs, the cause of much woe for pupils and teachers alike. However, such restraints should not deter those teaching, and in my role as a university tutor visiting primary schools I see many examples of fantastic work taking place to address thinking skills in problem-solving through dialogic talk in stimulating and inspiring lessons.

The legacy of the work of McGuinness and others is that thinking skills are very much in evidence in the 2014 curriculum for history, where children are required to 'think critically, weigh evidence, sift arguments and develop perspective and judgement' (DfE, 2013).

A holistic approach towards teaching history should also form a crucial part of our thinking when designing history lessons. A holistic approach to teaching is defined in any number of ways and encompassing spiritual, moral, social and physical themes. In addition, economic and cultural factors are often referred to when considering holistic approaches. In this way we can see a holistic approach to teaching as being concerned with developing the whole child.

Holistic learning encourages the development of a range of skills and competencies across these areas. Spiritual development can be seen as the ability to reflect upon your own actions and beliefs as well as the awareness to respect the beliefs of others. Moral development concerns itself with the ability to recognise right from wrong, consider actions and consequences, and to be guided by what is referred to in modern parlance as your 'moral compass'. This leads to making good choices and develops upright and reliable citizens. This links to the next aspect of social development. This involves the development of social skills in pupils, an awareness of community and the ability to operate and function within that community with an appropriate level of awareness of the self and the impact one has upon others. Physical development is concerned with the ability to look after, develop and understand one's own body, while economic development addresses the skills involved in looking after money, personal finances, running costs and an awareness of the function of money and the impact it has upon many aspects of life. Finally, cultural development involves an awareness of other cultures, the differences between cultures and the respect that that necessitates. This also relates to tradition and how history is formed and shaped.

Holistic learning refers to the idea that the whole child is considered in terms of both mind and body. Patel (2003) describes holistic learning as an approach that develops children to become more confident and independent and that recognises the importance of working on the self as well as social situations of learning. Lovat (2011) stresses that holistic learning is concerned with well-being.

Many of these areas can easily be linked to aspects of history that we have uncovered in this book, such as empathy, tolerance, the ability to see a situation from another point of view, to recognise the struggle that people in the past have faced and to identify how our view of life differs from that of people in the past.

So what should a history lesson look like? It can be argued that there is a time and a place for a more formal lesson, as there is for a lesson that requires writing. As always, a balanced approach is probably the best approach. This chapter has set out a series of ideas and principles concerned with the delivery of history lessons in the primary school. We have explored a number of factors, such as the use of objects, heritage learning, learning outside the classroom, thinking skills and holistic approaches, as well as considering approaches to teaching regarding discrete or cross-curricular lessons. There is a lot to consider, and we have not even looked at creative approaches.

There may be other factors that you will need to balance within your own context, such as whole-school policy, staffing and available resources and expertise. In addition to this, your own philosophy towards the teaching of history and how you see history in the classroom is of great importance. You should aim to be true to yourself and to what you know is good practice.

Reflection point

What is effective teaching of history? How will you structure your history lessons to ensure effective learning experiences that cover all the aspects of history?

Answer

The mystery object (Figure 3.2) is a Victorian pastry cutter, which would have been used to cut circles for scones and biscuits.

References

Alexander, R.J. (ed.) (2010) *Children, Their World, Their Education: Final Report and Recommendations of the Cambridge Primary Review.* Abingdon: Routledge.

Anderson, J. and Krathwohl, D. (eds) (2000) *A Taxonomy for Learning, Teaching and Assessing: A Revision of Blooms' Taxonomy of Educational Ojectives.* London: Pearson.

Bloom, B.S., Engelhart, M.D., Furst, E.J., Hill, W.H. and Krathwohl, D.R. (1956) *Taxonomy of Educational Objectives: The Classification of Educational Goals. Handbook I: Cognitive Domain.* New York: Longmans, Green.

British Museum and BBC (2013) A history of the world. 100 Objects that tell a story. *Primary History* 54.

Central Advisory Council for Education (1967) *Children and Their Primary Schools* (Plowden Report). London: HMSO.

Cooper, H. (2012) *History 5–11: A Guide for Teachers.* Abingdon: Routledge.

Davies, J. and Redmond, J. (2005) *Coordinating History across the Primary School.* London: Fulton.

De Bono, E. (1992) *Teaching Your Child to Think.* London: Penguin.

Dean, J. (2013) Urban spaces near you. *Primary History* 64.

Dean, J. and the Nuffield Primary History Project (2011) History in the curriculum: Overview. *Primary History* 57.

Department for Education (2013) *The National Curriculum for England.* London: DfE.

Department for Education and Skills (2006) *Learning Outside the Classroom Manifesto.* Nottingham: DfES.

Falk, J.H. and Dierking, L.D. (1997) School field trips: Assessing their long term impact. *Curator* 40(3): 211–18.

Feuerstein, R. (1980) *Instrumental Enrichment: An Intervention Program for Cognitive Modifiability.* Baltimore, MD: University Park Press.

Ginnis, P. (2002) *The Teacher's Toolkit: Raise Classroom Achievement with Strategies for Every Learner.* Carmarthen: Crown House Publishing.

Hickmott, K. and Chiasson, H. (2014) The new History National Curriculum: How to get the best from heritage. *Primary History* 68.

Historical Association (2011) Primary History Survey (England): History 3–11. http://www.history.org.uk/resources/primary_resource_8636.html (accessed 26 February 2016).

Hoodless, P. (2008) *Teaching History in Primary Schools.* Exeter: Learning Matters.

Lipman, M., Sharp, A. and Oscanyan, F. (1980) *Philosophy in the Classroom.* Philadelphia: Temple University Press.

Lovat, T. (2011) Special issue: Values education and holistic learning. *International Journal of Educational Research* 50(3): 145–146.

Maddison, M. (2014) The National Curriculum for History from September 2014: The view from Ofsted. *Primary History* 66.

McGregor, N. (2010) *A History of the World in 100 Objects*. London: Penguin.

McGuinness, C. (1999) *From Thinking Skills to Thinking Classrooms: A Review and Evaluation of Approaches for Developing Pupils' Thinking*. Research Report No 115. London: DfEE.

Mortimer, G. (2012) *A History of Football in 100 Objects*. London: Serpent's Tail.

Mortimer, G. (2013) *A History of Cricket in 100 Objects*. London: Serpent's Tail.

Ofsted (2011) *History For All*. London: Ofsted.

Patel, N.V. (2003) A holistic approach to learning and teaching interaction: Factors in the development of critical learners. *International Journal of Educational Management* 17(6/7): 272–284.

Piaget, J. (1936) *Origins of Intelligence in the Child.* London: Routledge & Kegan Paul.

Pickford, T., Garner, W. and Jackson, E. (2013) *Primary Humanities: Learning Through Enquiry*. London: Sage.

Turner Bisset, R. (2005) *Creative Teaching: History in the Primary School.* London: Fulton.

Wallace, B. (2003) *Using History to Develop Thinking Skills at Key Stage 2*. London: Fulton.

Wollins I.S., Jenson, N. and Ulzheimer, R. (1992) Children's memories of museum field trips: A qualitative study. *Journal of Museum Education* 17(2): 17–27.

4

Skills

One of the main objectives of this book is to raise awareness of what good history in the primary classroom looks like. We have already learnt that history goes far beyond the traditional view of the school subject and encompasses a wide range of aspects. We can see good history teaching as a balance between content and process. Historical knowledge and understanding, broadly speaking, constitute the 'content' of primary school history, while the 'process' of history is concerned with the mechanics of 'doing history' and being involved in enquiry and interpretation. This chapter and the next are concerned with two key principles: historical skills and historical concepts. In this chapter we focus upon the skills we wish to develop with our pupils as they engage in history lessons.

Historical skills are important as they develop critical reasoning and analytical skills. This may also include the capacity for solving problems, thinking creatively and justifying decisions. These are desirable attributes for children to possess.

Using historical skills, will see children engaging with questions and developing their own independent thoughts and opinions. This is best developed through the use of a range of artefacts, documents and countless other sources, both primary and secondary.

A key aim is for you to encourage children to think like historians. This will involve asking questions about what they want to find out about from the past: who, what, where, when, how and why? This will necessitate developing other skills, such as questioning the integrity of the evidence they are using and the reliability of the sources. Children should be encouraged to sift through evidence and make judgements as to what is relevant and what is not. It is both possible and advisable to devise activities that see the children developing historical skills and conceptual understanding simultaneously (see the next chapter for more on conceptual understanding). This may be the case especially when investigating empathy or the legacy of people from the past. In Chapter 1 we listed historical skills as observation, sequencing, analysing, understanding, questioning and synthesis and communication. Included here was also the development of historical vocabulary. At this point we can expand our understanding of historical skills and add thinking skills (both creative and evaluative thinking), reasoning and information processing.

Historical thinking, or thinking like a historian, develops historical understanding with our children regarding both the content and process of history. However, we need to identify two types of thinking here. The first of these is thinking as a historical skill. This is explicitly linked to enquiry although, as we will discover later in this chapter, we also need to identify a second type of thinking which refers more to a reflection on our findings and time to contemplate upon the meaning and impact. Both activities relate to 'doing' history. Hoodless (2008) discusses this type of information processing as a skill that aids chronological understanding, acknowledging that children need to process information in order to sequence events correctly. This form of thinking relates not only to sequencing activities, but also to other historical activities.

Vella (2010) advocates the use of artefacts in the classroom, which would, when used, require such processing skills in order for the children to form any kind of meaning. In her research, Vella (2010) sought to investigate the impact that learning strategies have upon cognitive development. She states that 'the most ordinary objects can yield much historical evidence'. Vella's intervention model recognised that the historical skills children displayed were impressive, observing that even the youngest of the children were making complex deductions. This led Vella to note that the thinking skills used in history are vital thinking skills. She also found that historical understanding in her study was socially constructed among groups of children and that this social interaction was vital to the children's development. This finding links to the way in which we learn. Bruner (1977) saw education and learning as the construction of new knowledge, with the 'act of learning' as a three-part process, starting with the 'acquisition' of new knowledge and moving to the 'transformation' of knowledge, before finally 'evaluating' the new knowledge. However, Vella's work links more obviously to the learning theory of socio-constructivism as advocated by Vygotsky (1978), who found that learning is constructed but also fired by significant others in the process. Vygotsky's 'zone of proximal development' would remain untapped if it were not for the structure and 'scaffolding' that 'experts' and 'more capable others' offer. The idea that discussion and constructed knowledge are important to learning is not new but it does serve as a reminder to practitioners to include time for such reflection, discussion and dialogic talk in our lessons.

Focused talk in history lessons will develop other historical skills, such as reasoning. Hoodless (2008) identifies reasoning as a historical skill. In order to practise reasoning, lessons need to incorporate time and opportunity for the children to talk to each other, share their thoughts and thrash around ideas before settling upon their 'reasoned' conclusions. This is another aspect of children's learning that is best developed through discussion, dialogue and with time to think and reflect. Of course, the nature of the discussions and the structured talk is up to the individual teacher who will know how best to address the needs of their learners, therefore discussions could look very different from one class to another according to the level of support and structure provided. The reasoning itself could take many forms. A mystery object, as we saw in Chapter 3, could be provided with the children left to wonder, discuss and reason as to what it may be. On another occasion, the validity of a source may be the topic for discussion. An account of a news item from a national newspaper compared to a regional newspaper, or a tabloid and a broadsheet, could provide much debate and discussion among the class if they identify any subtext, bias or hidden agenda within the articles. There are also links here to Philosophy for Children approaches and the work advocated by Society for the Advancement of Philosophical Enquiry and Reflection in Education (SAPERE).[1]

Sequencing relates to the concept of chronology that we will cover in more detail in Chapter 5. The skill of sequencing is of the upmost importance to the historian. In rationalising decisions, sequencing relates to the skill of reasoning and, as such, sequencing as a classroom activity can be used to address several other skills. Earlier in this book, I referred to old cameras that I have used in seminars and lessons. Initially, I use the cameras to draw observations (in itself another skill), encouraging children and trainees alike to come up with words to describe the cameras. We then move on to dating the cameras. This requires skills of deduction and sets the scene for other questions. Extra information can be provided at this point, such as 'Who was prime minister?' and 'Who won the FA Cup?', in order to investigate the world at the time that the particular camera was a new product. With a range of cameras, it is possible to create a timeline by challenging the class to order the cameras chronologically. Here, we are using a historical skill to develop a historical concept. Once sequenced, the children can be challenged to consider their reasoning. Why did they place one camera before another? As we saw earlier, such discussion and discourse can prompt a developing understanding. At this stage of an activity, the children may reaffirm their thoughts or be swayed to change their mind based upon the reasoning of one of their peers during the class discussion.

Davies and Redmond (2005) saw historical understanding as a skill. They identified that the 'range and depth of historical understanding' (p. 55) was concerned with 'not just knowing who, where, and when, but why' (p. 54). This is the crux of our understanding of what primary school history is all about. It is an important step away from textbook history which would provide a more than passable fact file for any given unit or topic of work, but an approach that seldom tackles the 'why' that is such an important aspect of what we know history to be today. In addressing this, schools will find themselves necessarily engaging in the 'process' of history and not just the 'content'. This perhaps goes some way towards highlighting the *History for All* report (Ofsted, 2011) findings that praised subject knowledge among children.

Another skill to be developed is that of interpretation. This could be confusing, as interpretation could be considered a concept. Here, however, we are distinguishing between the skill of interpreting and the conceptual understanding that there are interpretations and that differing views can and do coexist.

To truly address this aspect of history, children need to explore why some events are shown in certain ways and that events can be represented in different ways. Work in this area will also explore why this is the case, looking at the reasons why some interpretations of the past exist and how they came to exist. Such classroom activities may provide opportunities to question the reliability of some sources of evidence, which could lead to discussions about propaganda and bias.

Enquiry, as we have discovered, is a large part of what many educationalists and authorities recognise as being an essential aspect of good primary school history (Cooper, 2012; DfE, 2013; Maddison, 2014; Russell, 2015). This can be seen as 'doing' history, as opposed to being 'told' history as a story. Enquiry entails pupils investigating, sorting, retrieving, processing and sharing, all of which are integral to the body of

[1]http://www.sapere.org.uk/

historical skills. Enquiry involves the children questioning and analysing. This involves using sources and interrogating evidence, and combines with reasoning skills in order to produce findings, share conclusions and justify their interpretations. Hoodless (2008: 43) states that 'enquiry skills are the basic tools of the historian'. Hoodless also recognises that 'creative and evaluative thinking' is also 'required in the use of sources, forming conclusions from judgements' and the 'personal interpretations of events', concluding that the 'outcome of developing all these skills is the ability to solve problems and to "do" history' (p. 43)

Using source materials and artefacts allows children to explore objects and raise their own questions. This is an approach to using artefacts in the classroom that will create natural lines of enquiry that are raised from the children's own curiosity. Vella (2010) supports this approach, arguing that for younger children a hands-on approach with artefacts negates their less developed reading and writing skills. This allows younger children to engage with the process of 'doing' history without any hindrance. This reasoning applies to older children, too, the difference being that when it comes to articulating ideas or thoughts or to sharing findings, they have more options open to them.

Pickford et al. (2013: 12) notes that there is a 'considerable overlap between thinking skills and enquiry', arguing that they are practically the same thing. Certainly we can see how overlaps occur within investigations that engage the children in activities that require processing, reasoning, creative thinking and evaluation. We can also see, using Bloom's taxonomy (Bloom et al., 1956), how 'doing' history and the skills involved build upon each other, starting from the lower stages of 'knowledge' and 'comprehension' and building up to the higher stages of 'synthesis' and 'evaluation'. Children are engaged with building and developing historical skills from asking important who, what, where, when, how and why questions and then working with their findings to construct information, dispute evidence and justify assertions.

When considering the types of historical skills to address in lessons, the New South Wales Department of Education and Training (2010) provides an alternative view and sets out a broad range of areas to cover different types of history skills in the history syllabus for ages 7–10. These skills are identified as comprehension, analysis and use of sources, perspectives and interpretations, emphatic understanding, research and communication. Unpacking this further, we see familiar themes emerging. For comprehension skills, three areas are identified: to be able to read and understand texts, to use historical terms and concepts in appropriate contexts, and to sequence events within specific periods of time and to be able to explain continuity and change over time. This leads to the specific skills under the heading of 'analysis and use of sources'. Here, pupils are expected to identify different types and varieties of sources, identify the content, origin, purpose and context of historical sources, use and evaluate historical sources for historical enquiry, draw conclusions about the reliability and integrity of sources, and distinguish between fact and opinion. For 'perspectives and interpretations', the resource outlines specific skills as being able to identify perspectives of different individuals and groups and to recognise that historians themselves can interpret events differently. 'Emphatic understanding' requires the children to be able to interpret history within the context of actions, values, attributes and motives of people from the past. The skills relating to research identify the ability to plan historical research to suit the needs and purpose of an investigation and to locate, select and organise information from a variety of sources. The final section, 'Communication', requires the children to select the appropriate form of communication for specific purposes, to communicate effectively using oral, written, computer-based and other forms appropriate to a historical investigation and to use knowledge, understanding and relevant evidence to create appropriate historical texts.

This alternative breakdown of historical skills and attributes further consolidates our understanding of what historical skills are and what their function is. We can see that there is a combining of skills and concepts within this analysis and that such a binding of the two is necessary when involved in the processes of finding out about the past. Our understanding of the past is established and informed by the use of these skills in order to make sense of sources, understand motives and to develop a wider appreciation of the past with consideration of concepts such as change and the ability to acknowledge the process of history.

This breakdown of historical skills from the New South Wales Department of Education and Training (2010) is similar to the work of Byrom (2014) who also provides a useful overview of skills required at Key Stages 1 and 2. At Key Stage 1, Byrom identifies historical skills as an awareness of the past and the ability to use words and phrases relating to time. The ability to sequence people and events into chronological order is also listed, as is the identification of similarities and differences between different eras. The use of historical vocabulary and the ability to ask and answer questions are included, as is the ability to select sources in order to support ideas and demonstrate understanding. Key Stage 1 children should also demonstrate a knowledge of some of the ways in which the past is represented.

At Key Stage 2, Byrom stipulates that children engage with developing their chronological understanding of the past, as well as creating clear narratives across the periods and topics being studied. Children should be able to identify trends and contrasts and raise and address historically valid questions, as well as understand how knowledge of the past is constructed from a range of sources. Children should have the skill to construct their own ideas about the past based upon their use of sources, understand that different versions of the past exist and know why this might be the case. Byrom acknowledges that the ideas here are derived from the curriculum document itself, pointing out that the last point at Key Stage 2 is an unwritten progression from Key Stage 1. It is also clear from Byrom's work that, as with the New South Wales resource, skills and concepts are intrinsically linked. This is perhaps not surprising. As we have seen, historical skills are often employed in order to address historical concepts and the children's conceptual understanding of history.

Byrom (2014) refers to 'content' and 'skills' as phrases used widely among history teachers. Byrom would prefer to use the phrase 'historical knowledge' rather than 'content', but is clear that even this term would lead to confusion as knowledge is more than just the ability to recall people and events of the past. The term 'skills', Byrom says, causes still more confusion if used incorrectly, as it refers not only to historical skills such as research and communication, but also to 'thought processes' that involve organising ideas and recognising concepts. For this reason, I prefer to use the phrases 'content' for the subject knowledge of history, and 'process' for the understanding of the process of history.

Considering skills and good historical practice highlights the progression that we wish to see in developing our children's historical understanding. Byrom (2014) is keen to point out that aspects of history need to be developed together in order to enhance opportunities for historical understanding. Such an integration of skills and processes of history needs to be designed and planned before the teaching begins. This not only is good practice but will also avoid history lessons in schools becoming too fact based and falling into the trap of those lessons from yesteryear.

Skills progression

The skills progression table (Table 4.1) highlights the progression of skills and attributes associated with historical knowledge and understanding, chronological understanding, enquiry, historical interpretation and communication and organisation.

The intention of the skills progression table is to help structure learning experiences that ensure children revisit aspects and build upon their prior knowledge in order to progress to the next step as they move through their primary education. A further use of the table is to support you as the teacher in your assessment and monitoring of individual children within your class.

Toolkit ideas

The remainder of this chapter provides a selection of toolkit ideas that offer some helpful starting points for teaching primary history at Key Stages 1 and 2, specifically addressing the development of historical skills. More toolkit ideas can be found in later chapters.

Toolkit idea 4.1

Out of time

Skill: Observation

This is a simple activity that will quickly engage the children in the skill of observation, whilst focusing their thinking on a number of concepts, such as change, or in this case, anachronisms.

This activity requires the children to look closely at an artefact or other source such as the adapted image of the construction workers having lunch on a girder high above the New York skyline. I found the image via www. worth1000.com, but a simple Google search for 'photographs containing anachronisms', will supply similar resources for you to use. Honing this skill in such a fun way will enable the children to transfer their skills and apply the same techniques effectively and efficiently to other sources they encounter in other areas of historical investigation.

Table 4.1 Skills progression table

Aspect	Skills/ Attributes	Step 1	Step 2	Step 3	Step 4	Step 5
Knowledge and Understanding	Describe	Pupils have an emerging knowledge of stories of the past.	Pupils have a developing understanding of how people's lives have shaped our nation and the wider world.	Pupils have an understanding of aspects of British history and that of the wider world.	Pupils have a developed knowledge and understanding of the past and can articulate their understanding effectively.	Pupils can relate their understanding and underpin their ideas through a detailed knowledge of the past.
	Explain (links to Enquiry)	Pupils, when prompted, can explain how they know about the past.	Pupils can begin to explain their knowledge and understanding of the past in terms of evidence and sources.	Pupils can explain their knowledge and understanding of the past and how they found out about the past.	Pupils can explain in detail their knowledge and understanding of the past, including how they used sources of information.	Pupils can effectively explain how they gained their knowledge and understanding of the past.
	Compare/ Make Links	Pupils, when prompted, can compare the present with the past.	Pupils begin to demonstrate the ability to compare periods of history.	Pupils can compare periods of time in the past.	Pupils can compare different periods of time, making specific links to aspects of history, including historical concepts and attitudes.	Pupils can compare specific aspects of life in the past in different periods of time, paying particular attention to aspects of history, such as culture or economic implications.

(Continued)

Table 4.1 Skills progression table   (*Continued*)

Chronological Understanding	Concepts	Pupils are aware of concepts such as 'then and now' and change.	Pupils have a developing understanding of concepts of history, such as similarities and differences.	Pupils think about their knowledge and understanding of the past with reference to their conceptual understanding of history.	Pupils have an understanding of history in terms of historical concepts which include cause, consequence, significance as well as simpler concepts such as 'then and now'.	Pupils have a sophisticated knowledge and understanding of history and can effectively organise their thoughts in terms of historical concepts.
	Vocabulary	Pupils have an emerging vocabulary that relates to the passing of time.	Pupils have a developing vocabulary that relates to the passing of time.	Pupils use terminology associated with time and specific periods of history.	Pupils use an increasingly accurate vocabulary to emphasise their understanding of chronology.	Pupils use a sophisticated vocabulary to convey their deep understanding of chronology.
	Sequence	Pupils can identify old and new objects.	Pupils can place objects and events in chronological order.	Pupils can order artefacts, objects and events in chronological order.	Pupils can recognise features of periods of the past.	Pupils can recognise specific features of periods of the past with increasing accuracy.
	Reasoning	Pupils can recognise differences between the present and the past.	Pupils can begin to provide a rationale for their sequencing.	Pupils can provide a rationale for the sequencing of their artefacts, objects and events.	Pupils can support their chronological understanding through developed reasoning.	Pupils can argue and support their assertions through reasoned discussion.

Table 4.1 Skills progression table *(Continued)*

Enquiry	Enquiry/Use of Sources	Pupils can answer simple questions using sources from the past.	Pupils make simple observations and answer questions about the past.	Pupils can use different sources of information (including primary sources) in order to answer questions and draw conclusions.	Pupils are able to select information from different sources and explain what this tells us about life in the past.	Pupils are able to identify and evaluate sources of information and use these to reveal what life was like in the past.
	Questioning	Pupils can ask simple questions about the past.	Pupils can both ask and answer questions about the past using artefacts and other sources.	Pupils pose historically valid questions about the past.	Pupils can pose historically valid questions that underpin their knowledge and understanding of the past.	Pupils pose insightful questions that convey their deep understanding of the past.
Historical Interpretation	Reasoning	Pupils, when prompted, can make links between the artefacts they are using and the times that they belong to.	Pupils can make links between the artefacts they are using and the times they belong to.	Pupils can explain what artefacts and other sources tell us about the past.	Pupils can support their ideas about the past with reference to artefacts and other sources.	Pupils can argue and support their assertions about life in the past using artefacts and other sources.
	Interpretation	Pupils, when prompted, can recognise some of the ways in which life in the past is represented.	Pupils begin to recognise some of the different ways in which life in the past is represented.	Pupils recognise some of the different ways in which life in the past is represented.	Pupils know that some people and events in the past have been represented in different ways and can identify reasons for this.	Pupils understand and can describe and analyse why different versions of events exist.

(Continued)

Table 4.1 Skills progression table   (Continued)

Communication and Organisation	Explaining and Reasoning	Pupils, with support, can recognise that two accounts of an event may exist.	Pupils begin to recognise that two accounts of an event may exist.	Pupils can explain why differing versions of the past exist.	Pupils can explain why different accounts of the past may exist and the reasons for this.	Pupils can, with increasing effectiveness, explain why different accounts of the past may exist and the reasons for this.
	Select	Pupils, when supported, can begin to select appropriate historical information.	Pupils select appropriate historical information.	Pupils can select appropriate historical information to support a statement about the past.	Pupils can select appropriate knowledge and understanding of the past in order to discuss specific aspects of life in the past.	Pupils can select appropriate knowledge and understanding of the past in order to put forward an argument, support a point or offer an alternative view about the past.
	Organise	Pupils, with support, can begin to organise their knowledge and understanding of the past.	Pupils can organise their knowledge and understanding of the past into individual points.	Pupils can organise their knowledge and understanding of the past in terms of significance, importance and relevance.	Pupils can organise their knowledge and understanding of the past in order to discuss specific aspects of life in the past.	Pupils can effectively organise their knowledge and understanding of the past in order to put forward an argument, support a point or offer an alternative view about the past.

Table 4.1 Skills progression table (*Continued*)

Communicate	Pupils, with support, can communicate their growing knowledge and understanding of the past.	Pupils can communicate their knowledge and understanding of the past.	Pupils can communicate their knowledge and understanding of the past with a particular focus on an aspect of history or theme.	Pupils can communicate their knowledge and understanding of the past in a balanced manner that incorporates differing views of the past.	Pupils can communicate their deep understanding of the past that includes a balanced view of events of the past and a critical evaluation of historical sources.
Present	Pupils can write simple sentences, and talk, about their knowledge and understanding of the past.	Pupils can present their knowledge and understanding of the past in chosen forms.	Pupils can present their knowledge and understanding of the past in a variety of forms.	Pupils present their knowledge and understanding of the past in a variety of forms and include an appreciation of other points of view.	Pupils effectively present their knowledge and understanding of the past in a variety of forms and include an appreciation of other points of view and an awareness of how different accounts of the past exist.

Toolkit idea 4.2

Boudicca's appearance

Skill: Weighing evidence

I first encountered this activity at the Historical Association Conference in York a few years ago. Children here are presented with a sheet containing a number of images of Boudicca. Some of these images are statues, while others consist of paintings and clip art cartoons. Alongside the images is the account from Dio of Boudicca's appearance. The task is for the children to compare the sources and order the images in terms of reliability based upon Dio's account.

There is also the opportunity here to develop this work to include an examination of Dio's evidence. Why does a Roman describe Boudicca in such a way? What are the factors that have led to this account being adopted and shared?

Toolkit idea 4.3

Read all about it

Skill: Using artefacts to weigh evidence

Using newspapers is an interesting way to examine the past. Not only are the adverts, style of writing and tone interesting, but also newspapers themselves becoming a less and less familiar sight. For this activity you will need to source newspaper articles or the newspapers themselves, ideally newspapers containing reports upon the same event. For instance, another Google search will help you source articles from a range of newspapers regarding an event such as the sinking of the *Titanic*, Dunkirk, or an event that is particularly relevant to your unit or topic in your area.

The children then set about finding similarities and differences in the articles, distinguishing between facts and opinions across the papers and drawing their own conclusions about the events covered in the stories.

Toolkit idea 4.4

The camera never lies

Skill: Interpretation, weighing evidence

This is another activity encouraging children to interrogate evidence. While compiling this section for the book, I was reminded of a photograph of the Prime Minister, David Cameron, during the election campaign in 2015. The photograph that was released at the time showed him at a rally in Chippenham. He looked passionate as he spoke and was clearly connecting with the crowd of supporters that surrounded him. However, another photograph emerged that was taken at the same event, which revealed that, rather than being surrounded by a troop of loyal supporters, he was actually in a vacuous-looking warehouse surrounded by a small number of people huddled close by. This activity serves to prove that evidence needs to be interrogated, questioned and thoroughly analysed before being believed. The images can be found online.

Toolkit idea 4.5

'Snap' in place

Skill: Sequencing

This lesson idea involves sequencing a series of photographs into chronological order. Suitable photographs could consist of almost anything (irons, toys, etc.), but a collection of old photographs of the local area, such as the same street, would be ideal. Similarly, the same activity can be applied to different types of photographs, for instance, whole-class school photographs, team photos from your local football club or the royal family on the balcony of Buckingham Palace. The royals are regularly photographed together at the Trooping of the Colour as well as at significant national occasions and family events. These photographs could be sequenced in chronological order, with the children required to provide a reasoned justification for their choices. The photographs would see the coming and going of some royals, hair receding and royals ageing. The task will enhance the skills of observation as well as addressing weighing evidence, reasoning and concepts of chronology, change and continuity.

Toolkit idea 4.6

Interview

Skill: Questioning, enquiry

As we have identified, questioning is a historical skill at the heart of enquiry, and as with other skills, it needs to be practised and honed. Providing opportunities to ask valid historical questions can refer to questioning evidence and asking questions about artefacts and their reliability. However, questioning also means that the children can find out information through talking to people. Oral history is an aspect of history that we can develop here. Interviewing local people and asking them questions about their lives and the changes they have seen in the area that they share with the children is a powerful experience. However, the children need to be primed for such an activity. They need to know how to ask historically valid questions rather than 'what did you have for tea?' questions, although that is interesting too! Similarly, the children will learn to ask open questions rather than closed questions. For instance, asking 'were you scared during the war?' is likely to elicit a one-word, yes or no, answer, whereas asking 'do you remember what it was like during an air raid attack?' paves the way for a more detailed answer. With practice, the children can ask focused questions that reveal much about the past.

Toolkit idea 4.7

The ideas box

Skill: Interpretation, thinking, questioning, reasoning

This activity idea challenges the children to interpret the findings of an archaeological discovery. Materials are available at http://www.wessexarch. co.uk and cover the findings and the context of the discovery of the Amesbury Archer. Further information can also be found via the BBC website. However, the mechanics of the exercise can be applied to any activity.

The children are supplied with a range of sources, information, photographs and materials about a specific incident or event, in this case the discovery of the Amesbury Archer, and their task is to collate their findings and thoughts. A useful way of doing this is for the children to write into an ideas box. For group work this could be a large A3 size piece of paper, while for individual work a more manageable A4 piece would be sufficient. Rather than writing ideas onto a blank piece of paper, the children write into an 'ideas box' that is drawn on the paper. This eliminates the fear of 'getting it wrong' and the pressure of finding the answers, as work at this stage is all about collecting ideas and thoughts with no particular right or wrong responses. The children can be challenged to consider things they know and things that might be true. They could be prompted to make notes about how they know something and what has prompted them into that line of thinking.

The children can then move on to answering questions about the Amesbury Archer: Was he a king? What was he doing in Wiltshire? How old is he? The children can use their notes to find supporting evidence in order to answer the questions.

Toolkit idea 4.8

What was it like here long ago?

Skill: Sequencing, questioning

Documentary evidence engages the children quickly; this is especially true when looking at old maps. Such resources, particularly when looking at a local area, or an area the children know well, allow the children to explore the past from another perspective. This time the story is told by a succession of maps that depict an ever-changing landscape, which may include change in land use, urbanisation and the story of the development of their village, town or city. Maps are, of course, copyrighted materials, but some are available through different organisations. In Lancashire, for example, a team working at the Record Office can supply maps of the local area free of charge. There are an increasing number of apps and online services that allow you to access old maps, although there may be a charge involved. A feature here is that maps can easily be overlaid upon one another, making the changes clear for all to see. Historic England also provides teaching packs consisting of maps and other sources, both as bespoke packs for a specific school or more general packs for specific areas that will appeal to a wider audience, such as the pack on the Liverpool Docks. These are excellent resources that can be tweaked and adapted to suit the specific needs of your class.

Toolkit idea 4.9

Invaders

Skill: Understanding, reasoning through dialogic talk

We have identified understanding as a skill which children will need opportunities to develop. One way to address this is to provide questions that the children can discuss. For example, why did the Romans invade Britain? This would lead to developing historical knowledge (content) in that the children would find out that the Romans invaded three times, they would discover the dates and locations of each landing as well as a range of other information on the Romans in Britain. Understanding can be developed here in terms of investigating (process) why the Romans invaded on each occasion. Children will need to sift through sources in order to derive a list of considered reasons. Red herrings could be included by the teacher in order to challenge the children to consider the reasons for invasion. Work in this area would also move towards considering the Roman accounts of the invasions. The importance of dialogic talk can be emphasised here too. The children would be required to support their assertions and argue against other considerations.

Toolkit idea 4.10

History detectives

Skill: Thinking skills

In this chapter we have seen how thinking skills can be considered as 'creative' thinking skills and 'evaluative' thinking skills. This activity aims to develop both areas, requiring the children to be both creative in their thinking and considered in their responses.

For this activity, children are provided with a clue card containing several images relating to a particular person or event. For example, I have created a clue card that contains images of the Stars and Stripes, the state of Ohio, the moon, *Apollo 11*, Buzz Aldrin and a newspaper from 20 July 1969 (Figure 4.1), all of which should point to the mystery person being Neil Armstrong.

This, in essence, is a similar exercise to the suitcase activity. The children are developing the creative thinking by generating and extending ideas and hypothesising as they consider each clue. They also develop their evaluative thinking as they reason and rationalise their thoughts in order to draw their conclusions and reveal who they think the card refers to.

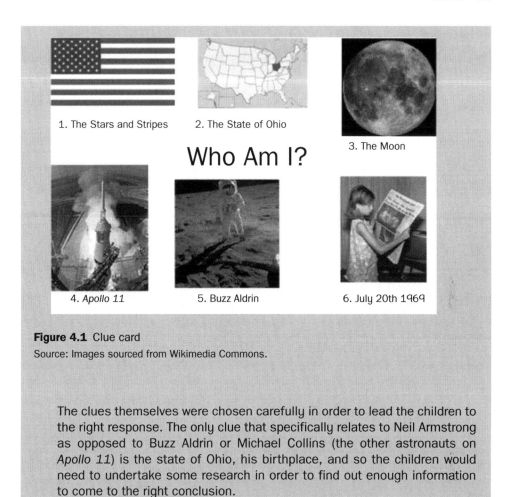

1. The Stars and Stripes   2. The State of Ohio

Who Am I?   3. The Moon

4. *Apollo 11*   5. Buzz Aldrin   6. July 20th 1969

Figure 4.1 Clue card
Source: Images sourced from Wikimedia Commons.

The clues themselves were chosen carefully in order to lead the children to the right response. The only clue that specifically relates to Neil Armstrong as opposed to Buzz Aldrin or Michael Collins (the other astronauts on *Apollo 11*) is the state of Ohio, his birthplace, and so the children would need to undertake some research in order to find out enough information to come to the right conclusion.

The purpose of this section is to provide a springboard of ideas in order to address historical skills that we have looked at in this chapter. Most practitioners will prefer to adapt and develop their own ideas, often using toolkit ideas such as these as starting points for bespoke activities for their own class.

Reflection point

What steps will you take to ensure that your lessons incorporate opportunities to develop historical skills?

References

Bloom, B.S., Engelhart, M.D., Furst, E.J., Hill, W.H. and Krathwohl, D.R. (1956) *Taxonomy of Educational Objectives: The Classification of Educational Goals. Handbook I: Cognitive Domain*. New York: Longmans, Green.

Bruner, J. (1977) *The Process of Education*. Cambridge, MA: Harvard University Press.

Byrom, J. (2014) *Progression in History under the 2014 National Curriculum. A Guide for Schools*. London: Historical Association.

Cooper, H. (2012) *History 5–11: A Guide for Teachers*. Abingdon: Routledge.

Davies, J. and Redmond, J. (2005) *Coordinating History across the Primary School*. London: Fulton.

Department for Education (2013) *The National Curriculum for England*. London: DfE.

Hoodless, P. (2008) *Teaching History in Primary Schools*. Exeter: Learning Matters.

Maddison, M. (2014) The National Curriculum for History from September 2014: The view from Ofsted. *Primary History* 66.

New South Wales Department of Education and Training (2010) *History for Those New to Teaching the Subject*. Sydney: NSW Department of Education and Training.

Ofsted (2011) *History For All*. Manchester: Ofsted.

Pickford, T., Garner, W. and Jackson, E. (2013) *Primary Humanities: Learning Through Enquiry*. London. Sage.

Russell, C. (2015) History. In M. Webster and S. Misra (eds), *Teaching the Primary Foundation Subjects*. Maidenhead: Open University Press.

Vella, Y. (2010) Extending primary children's thinking through the use of artefacts. *Primary History* 54.

Vygotsky, L.S. (1978) *Mind in Society*. Cambridge, MA: Harvard University Press.

5

Historical concepts

What are historical concepts?

This chapter will set out to explore historical concepts and how they can be addressed in the classroom. Throughout this chapter, we will explore what historical concepts are, how concepts are addressed in the classroom and how they relate to the historical skills we investigated in Chapter 4.

Concepts are important to what history is, and historical concepts are an important aspect of the teaching that takes place in history. Concepts in history help catalogue our knowledge and understanding and make sense of what we know about the past. Investigating historical concepts may include challenging children to make deductions and to classify their understanding in terms of change, continuity, similarity, difference, evidence, provenance, cause, effect, chronology and, to some extent, interpretation, although, as we saw in Chapter 4, interpretation can be seen as a skill. Each concept allows us to make sense of what we know and begin to understand where, in space and time, that knowledge fits into 'the big picture'. This chapter will explore ways in which schools address historical concepts and, in particular, that most imposing of historical concepts, chronology.

It is well documented that chronology is an aspect of history that has been overlooked in recent years (Ofsted, 2011; Maddison, 2014; Cooper, 2012). However, as we have discovered, the change in the curriculum has brought chronology to the forefront and therefore you will need to address and monitor your children's understanding of chronology in much more detail. The 2014 curriculum requires children to:

> understand historical concepts such as continuity and change, cause and consequence, similarity, difference and significance, and use them to make connections, draw contrasts, analyse trends, frame historically-valid questions and create their own structured accounts, including written narratives and analyses. (DfE, 2013)

Here, we can see that there is a clear link between conceptual understanding (continuity, change, cause, similarity, difference) and historical skills (make connections, draw contrasts, frame questions).

Providing opportunities to talk about historical concepts is an essential aspect of our history teaching. Indeed, opportunities for dialogic talk generally are an essential part of good primary teaching (Alexander, 2008). Such experiences provide opportunities for children to develop holistically in terms of their understanding of spiritual, moral, physical and economic issues. This, it could be argued, is especially the case when examining historical perspectives. A question such as 'which period, in British history, would you most like to have lived in?' may elicit an initial response from your class such as 'the Romans' or 'the Victorians', for example, which would be sensible answers. However, a true response to this question needs to be further qualified by consideration of the level of affluence you would experience in your preferred time. And living in any era would, of course, be much more rewarding and comfortable if you were rich. By providing opportunities to consider such ideas as affluence, we are developing the children's understanding of historical concepts as well as developing their attitudes and values. Considering different perspectives and life experiences is an important part of developing the whole child in a holistic way and also in developing their conceptual understanding of history.

An ability to engage with such thought processes is often affected by the experiences of each individual child. For example, it could be argued that a child whose family incorporates days out to museums and historical sites will be far better placed to engage in conceptual understanding in their learning than a child who has not had such experiences. This statement is merely intended to highlight that external factors, such as expectation and background, are likely to impact on the learner and their ability to learn. This discussion links to the debate surrounding the 'education gap' that considers attainment in comparison with expectation and background. Of course, the quality of the experience itself is key and can vary wildly. Quality conversation, questioning and discussion will add greatly to any learning experience. Hoodless (2008: 7) highlights how such interaction is a 'vital element of the learning process' in line with ideas put forward by Bruner (1977) as well as those of Bourdieu (1997) who identifies 'habitus' as a person's perception of their own place in the world and their ability to engage and interact in it.

An understanding of historical concepts is important for practitioners in order for them to effectively provide opportunities for their children to work with historical concepts in the curriculum. Progression in historical concepts is also important. In Table 5.1 concepts are set out in a clear progression across five steps. This sees children working from a position of being aware of historical concepts to being able to identify concepts, progressing to the point where they can think about their knowledge and understanding of historical information through their understanding of historical concepts, and then finally being able to organise their thoughts in line with their understanding of historical concepts. This last step, the organisation of historical concepts, builds on the work of Taba *et al.* (1971).

Hoodless (2008) sets out Taba *et al.*'s work nicely, highlighting how concepts in history can be split into two sets: 'organisational or methodological' concepts, which refer mostly to 'doing' history; and 'substantive' concepts which cover 'factual content' (Hoodless 2008: 12). Hoodless (2008) explains that 'organisational or methodological' concepts concern themselves with the organisation of our knowledge. For example, we might study the causes of the Great Fire of London and be able to group our responses

Table 5.1 Concept progression

Step 1	Pupils are aware of concepts such as 'then and now' and change.
Step 2	Pupils have a developing understanding of concepts of history, such as similarities and differences.
Step 3	Pupils think about their knowledge and understanding of the past with reference to their conceptual understanding of history.
Step 4	Pupils have an understanding of history in terms of historical concepts which include cause, consequence and significance as well as simpler concepts such as 'then and now'.
Step 5	Pupils have a sophisticated knowledge and understanding of history and can effectively organise their thoughts in terms of historical concepts.

into different types of reasons for the fire. In doing this, we have used the concept of causation. Hoodless (2008), using the example of Henry VIII and his six wives, demonstrates how a historian would also use the concept of effect if they not only considered the reasons for each of the six marriages (causation) but also considered subsequent events of each marriage (effect).

Cooper (2012) talks in terms of procedural concepts. These relate to the processes of history, and enquiry necessarily involves 'making deductions and making inferences from sources' (p. 41). In engaging with such concepts, learners can catalogue changes over time through concepts such as evidence, cause, effect, similarity, difference, continuity, change and interpretation. Further considerations would concern the reliability and validity of sources.

In order to address concepts, opportunities to develop skills and understanding in each area needs to be incorporated into schemes of work and become an embedded aspect of our work in history. Therefore, when we approach a new topic and are designing lessons, we need to find interesting and engaging ways to address concepts. For example, when looking at concepts of continuity and change, we can use a 1901 advert for the London Underground or Tube (Figure 5.1). This would fit nicely into a topic focusing upon 'transport' as 'an aspect or theme in British history that extends pupils' chronological understanding beyond 1066' (DfE, 2013).

By comparing the 1901 advert with a YouTube clip of commuters using the Tube, the children can easily identify aspects of change, continuity and similarities and differences. They can explore the reality of a trip on the Tube. This could include investigating the clothes worn by the people on the poster, who look as though they are going to the theatre for the evening, and drawing comparisons with modern clothes. Another approach may be taken here, too. Children could study a current advert for the Tube, which could be compared in a similar way. This may lead to work in other areas such as literacy and persuasive writing as well. As the poster is an advertisement, there are opportunities to discuss the reality of the scenes depicted in it and the overall validity of the source.

Figure 5.1 Tube advertisement

One artefact can be used to address several historical concepts. How these concepts are addressed and at what depth is down to the individual teacher and the needs of their class. The progression of conceptual understanding should help with mapping a cohesive pathway for the children and help monitor their experiences in working with historical concepts throughout their time at primary school.

As we have identified, chronology is an important historical concept to address. Hoodless (2008) asserts that the development of historical concepts begins at a very early age with, for example, routines such as feeding and bedtime instilling an understanding of the passing of time. This is further developed through weekly events, such as swimming lessons and play group, and through annual events such as family celebrations, holidays, birthdays and the marking of religious holidays. Throughout children's lives, then, the passing of time is experienced. Therefore the link between events and chronological understanding is a natural progression or extension of children's experiences in life. As Hoodless (2008: 7), states, learning about historical chronology is 'a further development of the process of learning about time that has been taking place in children's experiences since birth'. The use of timelines is traditionally the way most schools explore time, at least initially. This is a good way of developing chronological knowledge of a topic or a period of time.

The 2014 curriculum requires children to engage in 'a study of an aspect or theme in British history that extends pupils' chronological understanding beyond 1066' (DfE, 2013). This is intended to help address chronological understanding in the classroom and can be seen as an impact of the *History for All* report (Ofsted, 2011), which found that although primary school pupils had a good understanding of the topics they were studying, they had a less secure understanding of chronology. This unit is hence designed specifically to enable schools to study eras beyond 1066 and, at the same time, to also address chronology through a chosen aspect or theme. Those suggested within the document are non-statutory and consist of:

the changing power of monarchs using case studies such as John, Anne and Victoria, changes in an aspect of social history, such as crime and punishment from the Anglo-Saxons to the present or leisure and entertainment in the 20th century, the legacy of Greek or Roman culture (art, architecture or literature) on later periods in British history, including the present day, a significant turning point in British history, for example the first railways or the Battle of Britain. (DfE, 2013)

Schools will undoubtedly interpret these as they see fit and with due consideration of their own locality and heritage. It is easy to imagine how a topic on 'leisure and entertainment' or 'railways' can become embedded as part of a school's primary history curriculum and long-term planning, while the more abstract ideas of 'monarchy' and 'power' could make interesting topics for study too. The only real specification is that the aspect or theme is taken from British history. I imagine that many schools will use this, along with the local study unit that goes beyond 1066, in order to include long famil-iar primary school topics such as the Tudors, the Second World War or the Victorians. But perhaps there is an option to combine these studies with a shared theme such as 'war', 'legacy', 'leaders' or 'industry' which could similarly all be used to address chro-nology. Perhaps there is also the option of exploring chronology through technology, cars or photography, or through a concept such as 'evidence'. This would necessitate an examination of how we find out about the past as well as how those methods them-selves have changed over time. As we have seen with the Tube advertisement, there are countless options for you to explore.

Previously there have been recognisable gaps in the primary history curriculum, which paid no attention, for example, to the intrigue of the Middle Ages or life in the seventeenth and eighteenth centuries, leading to understandable misconceptions and questions about the past (Cooper, 2012). In contrast, the 2014 curriculum gives you the opportunity to provide a more coherent view of the past. Certainly, at face value, the curriculum for history goes some way towards promoting chronology, taking children's knowledge from the Stone Age to 1066 at Key Stage 2. However, as discussed elsewhere in this book, the topics and units do not have to be taught in chronological order. So will this really address the issue?

Concerns with how chronology is taught in the classroom are expressed by Reynolds and Hodkinson (2011). They describe chronology as the 'air that history breathes', claiming that chronological understanding enables pupils to place their learning within the 'bigger picture' and better remember 'historical people, periods and events'. They see the decline in chronological understanding as, in part, the effect of vague phrases and language that is associated with teaching chronology, such as 'a long long time ago'. They highlight the need for effective chronology teaching, with teaching experi-ences that need to be 'carefully planned and reinforced through fast-paced and enjoya-ble activities'. Their solution advocates a three-step plan for addressing chronology in the classroom: planning; vocabulary; and finally, fast-paced and fun activities.

At the planning stage, specific chronological understanding objectives should be incorporated into lesson plans. In addition, explicit links can be made between chrono-logical understanding and historical enquiries. This will act as a constant reinforcement of chronological ideas and knowledge as the pupils explore new eras through their enquiries. Another recommendation at the planning stage is to reinforce chronological understanding within the wider context of their historical work. This could be achieved through the use of timelines, which, while once considered passé, have come back into vogue within the last ten years or so, so that timelines and timeline activities once again find themselves at the centre of classroom work. Both personal and shared timelines are advocated by Reynolds and Hodkinson (2011) who promote, for example, the idea of using timelines in assemblies, which will help children in the school to place their learning in history across the school years.

Another idea would be to include interactive timelines into displays, not only in the classroom but also in communal areas of the school such as the school hall, dining areas and corridors. Children can study them in 'grey areas' of the day and compute the distance between events and dates in periods they are studying. A purposeful timeline needs to be big, bold, clear and preferably interactive.

When considering the second point (vocabulary) in Reynolds and Hodkinson's (2011) three-point plan, we need to ensure that the language of chronology is clear and precise and used correctly and consistently. They state that there are three categories of vocabulary: 'descriptive vocabulary', 'technical vocabulary' and 'conceptual vocabulary'. Descriptive vocabulary consists of words and phrases such as 'before', 'after', 'ancient', 'old', 'new', decade', 'century', 'millennium' and 'modern'; technical vocabulary refers to 'AD', 'BC' and the use of 'ninteenth century' for 1845. Conceptual vocabulary refers to historical concepts, such as change, continuity, sequence, duration, period and chronology. Consistently accurate use of such terms is essential in providing an underlying understanding of chronology. Using such terms as these regularly will embed understanding and instil a confidence among the children to use such terms accurately themselves.

The final aspect of Reynolds and Hodkinson's three-step plan is the use of 'fast-paced and fun activities'. Their suggestions relate to the use of timelines. Timelines need to be purposeful in order to be meaningful and to have an impact upon the learning and chronological understanding that is taking place. Reynolds and Hodkinson (2011) suggest a teacher's timeline with photographs and events from the teacher's own life used to illustrate the passing of time. Such a revelation of personal information, while not sitting comfortably with some teachers, would certainly capture the children's imagination and interest. It also means that the children can compare dates with those of their own family and friends. Personal timelines can include photographs and the recording of special events in the lives of the children. These can be created in many ways, including washing lines, as well as a more regular paper version. You may like to explore the potential of apps and web-based tools for timelines to create with your class, such as those available on http://www.timetoast.com. Timelines can incorporate events from family and friends as well as their own. A word of caution here, though; when studying some aspects of family life, the teacher needs to be aware that not all families are the same and that not everybody is comfortable with sharing information about themselves, and therefore a degree of sensitivity is required at times.

From personal timelines, there is the scope to develop the timeline to include events that occurred before the children were born. These events could be of national and international significance or could solely be based upon the family, community of the school and local town. The contributions of others will develop a shared timeline and will serve to develop chronological understanding.

Much work on timelines uses the historical skills of sequencing. When you are designing your history lessons it is essential to provide a coherent experience.

Therefore, making links between the historical skills that you want to develop in the children and the historical concepts you want them to understand would seem like a sensible approach. In much the same way, the skill of questioning and asking perceptive questions relates to enquiry. Throughout the national curriculum for history (DfE, 2013) similar links between historical skills and concepts are made.

In addition to what we study here, we need to think about how we teach chronology. Toolkit ideas, at the end of this chapter, aim to provide a few starting points and classroom ideas that you can adapt, tweak and use in your own classrooms.

When considering the implementation of the teaching of concepts in the classroom, Cooper (2012: 43) proposes that concepts could be addressed through the teaching of strands, suggesting 'religion, homes, leisure, transport, conflict, art and music' as suitable strands. This is an interesting suggestion and is in line with the suggestions made in the curriculum itself. However, one concern may be that units could potentially become too formulaic and similar.

Identity

Identity as a concept is a really important aspect of history for us to consider here. The Cambridge Review (Alexander, 2010) recognised that the teaching of history is important in helping children understand who they are. The question 'who are you?' is at the centre of much of the thinking within the teaching of history. This notion was introduced in Chapter 1. History, and our understanding of our own history, is important in our understanding of ourselves, our sense of belonging and ultimately our own identity.

Throughout our lives we adopt several identities according to the situation. At school we adopt the identities of a pupil and a friend. At home we adopt other identities such as being a son and a husband. Developing a sense of understanding about how you, as an individual, operate and exist in the world can have a real impact upon understanding yourself as a learner, as a member of society, as a son, daughter or in any of the various roles that you inhabit and your place in the grand scheme of things.

This may seem a long way from primary school history and our traditional view of school history as being about topics, such as the Romans or the Anglo-Saxons, but increasingly an exploration of 'self' is intrinsically related to concepts of history such as evidence, provenance, and that 'sense of belonging' that we have also identified as being a part of history.

Consider this. What influences you as a person? What events have had a great impact upon the way you live your life? What influences your thoughts as to what is 'normal'? What are the expectations you have of yourself? Who or what influences these? What influences your outlook on life? Even the way you speak, the inflections in your voice, your mannerisms and tics have a starting point based in the factors that influence who you are. This, of course, relates to you professionally too. For instance, why did you want to be a teacher in the first place? What was the initial spark? How did your school experience affect you in terms of choices, options and expectations? Was this a result of where you lived and the school you went to, the area that you call home?

I pose these questions in order to emphasise the point that identity can be influenced by a wide range of factors. Of course, each individual can change particular factors and create new beginnings for themselves, but that in itself is a result of the influences that led you to that decision to make a determined change. We are all influenced by our family, our friends, their interests, by the films we watch and the books we read. Identity is the essence of who we are, and this applies to the children you teach as well. The identity you choose to share with others can also be seen as an aspect of each individual's identity. You may be selective in how you present yourself in some situations. For example, are you the same with your work colleagues as you are with your best friends? Do you adopt a 'telephone voice' in certain situations? Is there a professional you and a weekend you?

On a national scale, we act within our identities too. We share some events, such as the Olympics in 2012 or a royal birth as a collective national experience and respond accordingly. Some experiences will be more personal to individuals: the time your team won the FA Cup, for instance, was a shared experience for you and others and a memory that you hold dear. In addition, there are specifically personal events, such as family birthdays, anniversaries and dates that are significant to you. Equally, there are some occasions that collectively refer to events of the past that have a larger impact upon you than they might do on others. An example here might be the impact of the Hillsborough disaster. This refers much more closely to our personal histories that act as our own catalogue of our own past.

There is also a 'personal nostalgia' that influences us and shapes our interactions. We hold memories of people, places and events in our lives with great respect. This is demonstrated in the sentiment of the Beatles song 'In My Life', which is not only a beautiful love song but also a recognition of change, the past, and events and people. There is an acknowledgement that these people and places will always be special. Our understanding of the past, and our own past, is further shaped by mementos: our own personal museum of artefacts, the things we have collected along our way. A shoebox full of letters, a shelf of knick-knacks from long ago holidays, a teddy bear, a gift from a loved one, all such artefacts demonstrate our recognition of our past and its constant reminder on the present.

Our understanding of ourselves in place and time will also be influenced by those factors that we identified earlier in this book as part of a holistic approach to learning. One, some or all of social, economic, spiritual, cultural and moral factors may influence our identity and the identities we adopt in any given situation.

It can be argued that, in (certain strands of) society today it is not 'cool' to be seen to want to learn or even to be good at something or dedicated to something. For a pupil at school, peer pressure may lead them away from their interest in history or their passion for a hobby such as a musical instrument, with the desire to be accepted by their peers proving to be too much of a pull. Even at university, I have noticed how some trainees are unwilling to ask questions and pursue an idea further in seminars, only for them to wait until the end of the session or email later to continue their interest away from the prying eyes of their peers. I think this is not only a great shame, but also a manifestation of their awareness of their identity. In this case the identity of the learner is compromised by their need for social acceptance. This idea of being aware of yourself as a learner also relates to an understanding of how good you are as a learner. This may include internal discussions regarding metacognition, a determination to apply oneself and a disciplined approach to learning.

Identity involves mind, body and soul, and in this way an awareness of such can be addressed in the primary history curriculum. Personal timelines, local study units and developing empathy will address aspects of identity, understanding of themselves, a developing pride in their home town and an understanding of their place in the world. Development of these areas relates to work in primary history.

Toolkit idea 5.1

The history of ...

Concepts: Identity, evidence

This simple idea is to research something that you are interested in – for example, 'the history of the motorcar'. Encourage the children to consider things that they enjoy, whether a band, a book, a hobby or a pastime. Encourage the children, using their researcher skills, to investigate their chosen area and to use a number of sources wherever possible. In researching and then sharing their chosen area, the children are investigating their own identities and influences.

Toolkit idea 5.2

A day in the life of a 10-year-old

Concepts: Chronology, change, continuity, evidence

An interesting approach would be to explore what life was like for a 10-year-old at various points in British (and world) history. With this idea, the routines of a 10-year-old could be investigated. A series of such investigations could help address chronology, while individual investigations could be used to explore concepts such as change, continuity, similarities and differences. Investigating how we know would also address the concept of evidence.

Toolkit idea 5.3

Order, order

Concept: Chronology

Most approaches to chronology involve the use of a timeline. This practical idea for the classroom uses a timeline to help the children present and sort out their thoughts about the chronology of a topic. In this instance, the children are presented, in the form of flash cards, with a number of key events that are studied while exploring the *Baghdad AD 900* study unit. No dates are provided at this stage. The children are challenged to order the events and provide a reason and justification as the their answers. The teacher may choose to add some information to the discussions and to prompt as required. The children then share their sequences, attaching the flash cards to a timeline as they provide their rationale for the order they have positioned the cards. At this stage the teacher will monitor the arguments and the correct positioning, using the other groups and tables to prompt the discussion and keeping a check on the year that each event has been assigned. There is scope for this task to lead to further research and for the children to begin to form considered arguments for their decisions.

Toolkit idea 5.4

Stone, Bronze, Iron

Concepts: Enquiry, knowledge and understanding

This idea is concerned with sequencing events and developments and building subject knowledge. Children could be given a selection of 'facts' and key cards referring to the developments that occurred during the Stone, Bronze and Iron ages. These cards could include key facts about places early humans settled, such as Skara Brae, the development of trackways, the move from a nomadic form of society to a community based in one location and early farming. In sorting and ordering the cards, the children are demonstrating their knowledge and understanding and the teacher is providing opportunities for discussion and for a rationale for their choices to be conveyed. This activity could therefore, be used not only to share information but also to assess understanding.

Toolkit idea 5.5

Skara Brae

Concepts: Change, continuity, similarities, differences

Encourage the children to look at photographs of the homesteads at Skara Brae. Ask them what they notice. Move to labelling the areas within the homestead: fire, bed, shelves. Then discuss what life would be like around the fire, the food they would be eating and the hardships they might face. Then discuss what might be kept in the pots (spices, herbs, water) and what might be kept in the shelves and cubby holes that can be seen in the stone walls (prized possessions/valuable items). This could lead to a discussion about prized possessions and things that the children value. Draw comparisons between the items we would consider valuable and the items that the people of Skara Brae would have treasured (a sharp stone, a piece of leather)

Summary

In this chapter we have explored historical concepts. We have categorised concepts and looked at how concepts can be addressed in the classroom. We have looked closely at chronology and the 2014 history primary curriculum that 'aims to ensure that all pupils understand historical concepts such as continuity and change, cause and consequence, similarity, difference and significance' (DfE, 2013). We have made links to historical skills and the ability to 'make connections, draw contrasts, analyse trends and frame historically-valid questions'. This will result in the children being able to create 'structured accounts' and 'written narratives and analyses'. This chapter has also considered identity as a historical concept and the importance of historical understanding in understanding our own identity.

We have also looked at toolkit ideas that address historical concepts and can be used and tweaked to suit the needs of your class.

Reflection point

Why are historical concepts an important aspect of historical understanding and children's engagement with history?

References

Alexander, R. (2008) Culture, dialogue and learning: Notes on an emerging pedagogy. In N. Mercer and S. Hodgkinson (eds), *Exploring Talk in School*. London: Sage.

Alexander, R.J. (ed.) (2010) *Children, Their World, Their Education: Final Report and Recommendations of the Cambridge Primary Review*. Abingdon: Routledge.

Bourdieu, P. (1997) *The Love of Art* (new edition). Oxford: Polity Press.

Bruner, J. (1977) *The Process of Education* (new edition). Cambridge, MA: Harvard University Press.

Cooper, H. (2012) *History 5–11: A Guide for Teachers*. Abingdon: Routledge.

Department for Education (2013) *The National Curriculum for England*. London: DfE.

Hoodless, P. (2008) *Teaching History in Primary Schools*. Exeter: Learning Matters.

Maddison, M. (2014) The National Curriculum for History from September 2014: The view from Ofsted. *Primary History* 66.

Mercer, N. and Hodgkinson, S. (eds) (2008) *Exploring Talk in School*. London: Sage.

Ofsted (2011) *History for All*. Manchester: Ofsted.

Reynolds, A. and Hodkinson, A. (2011) How to teach chronology. *Primary History* 57.

Taba, H. *et al*. (1971) *A Teacher's Handbook to Elementary Social Studies: An Inductive Approach*. Reading, MA: Addison-Wesley.

6
Planning

In this chapter, we look at how the primary curriculum for history could be organised across Key Stages 1 and 2. This chapter maps out the 2014 curriculum and discusses the rationale for organizing the curriculum in various ways. In addition, this chapter explores planning for purposeful history lessons in Key Stages 1 and 2, ensuring that the aspects of the history curriculum are covered. This chapter also addresses the process of planning a scheme of work for a history topic, accommodating the skills progression table in Chapter 4. Approaches to teaching history, including using field trips, are also considered.

This chapter further considers the roles and duties of the history coordinator. The importance of history specialists is assessed in terms of working with clusters of schools, as well as sharing ideas within networks.

The secret to successful teaching and learning, as with most things in life, is preparation. For delivering meaningful learning experiences, this means planning structured lessons that address aspects of history that we identified earlier in this book. As we have seen over the previous two chapters, lessons often consist of a balance of the development of historical skills and historical concepts. Therefore, a series of lessons on a topic, such as the Romans, needs to be not only a balance of skills and concepts but also a balance between content and process. Lessons in a scheme of work need to provide opportunities to develop knowledge and understanding of not only the topic but also the process involved in historical enquiry. Another consideration is the aspect of communication. How will children communicate their new knowledge, and will this communication include both content and reference to the process? This will naturally provide opportunities for assessment, which we will explore further in the next chapter, but it is an important element of the planning stage that opportunities and the nature of the opportunities for communicating learning are included in lesson plans.

Lesson plans for 'Changes in Britain from the Stone Age to the Iron Age'

As an example, these lesson plans show a selection of lessons for the topic 'Changes in Britain from the Stone Age to the Iron Age' for a Year 3 class.

Year 3 Lesson Plan
Lesson 1: When was the Stone Age?
Aspect of history: Chronology

Learning Objectives	Teaching Activities	Children's Role	Resources/Notes	Assessment/Outcomes
When To locate the Stone Age, Bronze Age and Iron Age on a timeline of British history To understand how long the Stone Age, Bronze Age and Iron Age periods lasted To know that there are three eras within the Stone Age	**Challenge** children, in groups or pairs, to sequence flash cards of different periods of British history (differentiated in terms of dates, images, clues) **Explain** that the children must be able to provide a reason for their particular sequence **Prompt** discussion as the children work on the task **Make links** to eras that have been studied by the class previously **Discuss** with the children the correct order (children reorder where necessary) **Create** a class timeline **Locate** the Stone Age on the timeline **Note** that it is followed by the Bronze Age and Iron Age **Note** that this part of British history is sometimes referred to as 'prehistory' **Discuss** BC (or other terms such as BP) and locate when the Stone Age began (450,000 BC Palaeolithic Era) **Explain** that this unit will explore life in Britain (and other parts of the world) up to the end of the Iron Age (AD 43) **Explain** that the first few lessons will look at the Stone Age	Working in pairs Sequencing cards Create a class timeline	**Vocabulary** History, Chronology, Stone Age, Bronze Age, Iron Age, Palaeolithic, Mesolithic, Neolithic Archaeologist Evidence BC, AD **Resources** History of Britain timeline cards	Sequencing Timelines Evidence

Challenge the children to find when the Stone Age began (450,000 BC) and ended (around 2300 BC) Children **create** a timeline (or notes if you prefer) in their books that begins in 450,000 BC and ends in 10,000 BC. Explain that this period is called the Palaeolithic Era. Add 10,000 BC to 4500 BC to your timeline and label this the Mesolithic Era, and finally add 4500 BC to 2300 BC and label this as the Neolithic Era

Challenge misconceptions, such as dinosaurs/wheels

How do we know? Discuss how, through archaeology and archaeologists' work, we know when and where Stone Age man lived.

Using the timeline. Creating a timeline/notes in their books.

Year 3 Lesson Plan
Lesson 2: Where did Stone Age people live?
Aspect of History: Evidence

Learning Objectives	Teaching Activities	Children's Role	Resources/ Notes	Assessment/ Outcomes
Evidence: Where did Stone Age man live?	**Ask** How do we know where Stone Age man lived? Responses should refer back to Lesson 1 discussion	Answering questions	**Vocabulary** Evidence Proof	Sifting evidence
To explain how we know where Stone Age people lived	**Explain** that we want to investigate where Stone Age man lived. There is evidence of Stone Age man in northern Europe (such as Germany) but also closer to home	Collecting information		Conclusions
To know that there is evidence of Stone Age people in Britain and in our local area and in other parts of the world	**Did Stone Age man live in France?** Look at the Lascaux resource http://www.lascaux.culture.fr/?lng=en#/fr/00. xml		**Resources** Newspaper articles Books Internet	Answers to enquiry questions
To use evidence to support ideas and information	**Did Stone Age man live in England?** **Look** at evidence and children's prior knowledge (Stonehenge, stone circles, tools, flints, etc.), collection of newspaper articles			
To research topic to widen knowledge	**Did Stone Age man live in our local area?** **Share** newspaper articles and encourage children to collect information about the earliest evidence there is for Stone Age man Castlerigg Stone Circle Lunt. Evidence at Atkinson Gallery, Southport **Challenge** Using books/internet and work in other lessons, find the answers for these questions			

Questions (some will have been answered in other lessons)

What is the earliest evidence of Stone Age man in England?

Did Stone Age man live in Africa? Europe?

When was fire discovered?

Who were the Beaker people? (this will overlap with Bronze Age Britain)

Where did Stone Age man come from?

When did Britain become an island? c. 6000 BC Britain becomes separated from the European mainland

Following the end of the last Ice Age, around 10,000 years ago, the levels of the North Sea began to rise as waters formerly locked up in great ice sheets melted. Sometime after about 8200 BC the last dry 'land bridge' from Lincolnshire and East Anglia to Holland was taken over by salt marsh. By 6000 BC even the marshes had largely gone, drowned by the sea

What kind of house did Neolithic man build?

In which Stone Age era were ploughs first used?

Could Stone Age man store food?

When was the wheel invented?

Using the information gained with these questions, add the facts to the definitions of key features of the three Stone Age eras

For each new piece of information, add how we know (i.e. the source)

Year 3 Lesson Plan
Lesson 3: What did a Stone Age person's house look like?
Aspect of history: Change and continuity

Learning Objectives	Teaching Activities	Children's Role	Resources/ Notes	Assessment/ Outcomes
Skara Brae To know that Neolithic man made a homestead To know that different sources can produce conflicting findings To know that cultivating the land and farming led to Neolithic man settling in areas and creating trade routes	**Ask** What did a Stone Age person's house look like? Think about Neolithic houses. Last lesson we discovered that Neolithic man lived in rectangular cabins. Other sources tell us that Neolithic man lived in mud huts. However, we know that Neolithic man lived in a place in Orkney called Skara Brae. Perhaps all are true in different areas. Skara Brae What is your favourite possession? Where do you keep it? How is that different from where you keep other things? Where would Neolithic man keep his prized/valuable possessions? Tell the story of Skara Brae being (re)discovered in 1850 What was life like? BBC animation 'A day in the life of a 10-year-old boy in the Stone Age' https://www.youtube.com/watch?v=cE6OeRZB_Wc	Identifying examples of change and continuity.	**Vocabulary** Homestead Fire Bed Dresser Shelter Warmth Safe **Resources** Photographs of Skara Brae	Identified examples of change and continuity.

Year 3 Lesson Plan
Lesson 4: What is Stonehenge?
Aspect of history: Interpretation

Learning Objectives	Teaching Activities	Children's Role	Resources/Notes	Assessment/Outcomes
The Bronze Age Stonehenge To form ideas and thoughts regarding Stonehenge For the children to be able to explain how they found something out	**Create** a Stonehenge fact file **Challenge** the children to consider what they want to know about Stonehenge and then let them work in pairs to explore various sources in order to compile their own fact file about Stonehenge **What do we know about Stonehenge? What do we think Stonehenge was built for?** Work began on Stonehenge during the Neolithic Era but was completed during the Bronze Age (2500–2000 bc) http://www.stonehenge.co.uk/ceremony.php http://www.livescience.com/22427-stonehenge-facts.html http://www.softschools.com/facts/wonders_of_the_world/stonehenge_facts/92/ http://primaryfacts.com/1483/stonehenge-facts-and-information/ Possible activity: research British Museum web-site and other sources	Collecting Information Analysing Interpreting Writing	**Vocabulary** Stonehenge Structure Religion Solstice Belief Custom **Resources** Websites Books	Responses to the two enquiry questions Use of sources Children to explain how the they found out about Stonehenge

These four lessons, taken here from a complete scheme of work, highlight several areas within this chapter. The first lesson provides a context for the learning, and much of the work in the first lesson addresses chronology, setting the learning in context of the big picture. At this point it is important to address the idea of using correct historical terminology for the topic, such as prehistoric, BC, Stone Age, Neolithic and Mesolithic, as suggested by Reynolds and Hodkinson's (2011) work on chronology. Creating a class timeline is also an important aspect of addressing chronology and developing a sense of understanding regarding the placing of the Stone Age in the history of Britain.

Misconceptions, such as dinosaurs, wheels and other misplaced thoughts about the Stone Age period can be identified and addressed at this early stage of the topic and reinforced throughout the series of lessons. In fact, many teachers will build in opportunities to address misconceptions throughout a scheme of work, including opportunities to consolidate new knowledge and to question presumed knowledge. Through such class discussions areas for research and enquiry become apparent and you then have the opportunity to accommodate naturally arising areas of enquiry that have been identified by the children themselves. This provides the children with a sense of ownership over their work and harnesses their enthusiasm and curiosity. Enquiry, as we have seen, is a driving force behind much of history teaching and forms a fundamental aspect during the scheme.

The lessons shown here utilise a number of sources of evidence that allow the children to engage with historical skills and concepts as they explore the Stone Age era. In many cases the sources are likely to be in a digital format, determined by the nature of the topic and the format that is most readily available. However, wherever possible, a balance of approaches and experiences with sources is desirable. With a topic such as the Stone Age the location of your school will determine opportunities for field trips to prehistoric sites or access to museums with relevant collections, such as the reference to the Atkinson Museum in Southport in Lesson 2.

Over the course of a scheme of work, you should aim to provide a mixture of experiences in order to address aspects of history as well as the content and processes of history. In most cases the first lesson in a scheme of work will be used to set up the new topic. This may involve establishing a context for the work and establishing when in time the topic took place, therefore providing opportunities to address chronology. Using timelines and setting the work within existing knowledge, in terms of the position of the new topic in relation to topics previously studied, provides an opportunity for you to identify what the children already know about the topic. In many cases you may find that prior knowledge of a topic stems from popular culture such as *Horrible Histories*, in book, television, magazine and website guises. Similarly, children will encounter interpretations of the past in comics, cartoons, TV, films and video games. The cartoon of Scooby-Doo and the gang being chased by a cursed Egyptian mummy provides an example of how our encounters with the past are initially formed and shaped. Some children will have access to fact books and non-fiction texts about specific periods, perhaps a DK Eyewitness book or a '100 facts about' book. These books are fantastic resources to use in lessons that provide subject knowledge and the 'hooks' upon which we can hang our good history teaching. They can also be used to address other issues in primary education such as getting boys to read.

Setting the context for the study unit may also include identifying the areas of enquiry that you will want to tackle during the scheme of work as a whole. This is an opportunity to share with the children the planned investigations and areas of investigation that they will be exploring over the next term or half term. In planning terms, it is also an opportunity to ensure that there is a good coverage within the topic of skills and concepts that we have identified as good history. As we have seen, we want to ensure that the children encounter a good range of sources; however, we also want our study to cover areas such as change, continuity, and interpretations of history. In so doing, we are seeking to ensure that the children develop a range of skills as they study the topic. Logistically, individual teachers may spread this over an entire year and therefore over more than one topic or study unit. Certainly some elements might be more difficult to arrange and provide, such as learning experiences involving a relevant trip or a guest speaker. However other areas, such as chronology, may be addressed more frequently. The important thing here is to plan for the children to encounter all experiences and to ensure a good level of coverage and a balance of activities and foci for your lessons.

Children will not respond well to repetitive lessons that only require the same skills lesson after lesson, but will respond to interesting ways of presenting information or contexts for their enquiry in ways that help them to develop a range of skills. Lessons may require the children sometimes to work collaboratively, and at other times alone. Approaches to teaching history need to be set out at the planning stage, including the range of experiences that will be covered. Another consideration here is for the discussion regarding discrete or cross-curricular or topic teaching. In most cases, this will be a whole-school consideration. However, it is worth remembering the challenges in this approach highlighted by Ofsted (2011) and Maddison (2014) and the findings of the teacher survey (Jones, 2011) as discussed in Chapter 2.

When considering planning activities we must also consider assessment opportunities. We will discuss assessment further in the next chapter. Here we need to be aware of the importance of assessment and have an understanding of where it will fit in individual lessons as well as entire schemes of work. The cyclical nature of planning and assessment is long established in primary school practice. The idea of planning and delivering a learning experience also includes an aspect of reflection and evaluation. Kolb (1984) devised the most familiar planning cycle used by schools throughout the world.

Kolb's model highlights the importance of reviewing a teaching and learning experience in order to evaluate its effectiveness and consider future implications. Such a model also highlights the importance of short-term plans and the opportunity here to tweak plans to suit specific needs of individual children in your class, or to incorporate new opportunities that have presented themselves. Even new discoveries and topical news items can be incorporated into your plans, as was the case in 2009 when the discovery of the Staffordshire Hoard altered my history lesson plans for my Year 4 class.

Of course, we are jumping ahead here: short-term plans are the product of medium-term plans, which in turn are formed from the long-term plans a school will have in place.

Long-term plans

Long-term plans allow the school managers and staff to set out all the topics and curriculum areas that need to be taught across the primary age phases of Key Stages 1 and 2 and the academic year. At this stage, considerations such as the chronological delivery of the curriculum that we discussed in an earlier chapter and whether or not topics will be further developed, such as a study of the Romans, or indeed whether additional units, that perhaps suit individual schools, will be added to the curriculum. Other considerations, such as highlighting opportunities to discuss British values, could also be contemplated at this stage.

Long-term plans are usually the aspect of planning that are shared with parents via the school's website and handbook, giving parents and the children an indication as to the studies that lie ahead.

Medium-term plans

Individual schools will address medium-term plans differently, especially when considering the level of detail required at this stage of the planning process. To some schools, the medium-term plans are so in-depth and focused that there is little need for them to be adapted further. Different schools will hold different views on this. Some schools approach will regard medium-term plans as the point at which ideas, resources, trips and lesson structures will be thrashed out and fleshed out. This gives individual teachers the opportunity to organise school trips, finalise dates, organise helpers and book venues and coaches in good time, as well as addressing the need to cover the content and process of history lessons that we identified earlier. Learning objectives can be mapped out over a scheme of work to ensure coverage is taking place.

Short-term plans

There is an in-built contradictory aspect to the short-term plans, which are sometimes referred to as weekly plans. They are designed and written to contain details about the planned teaching and learning activities for individual lessons in minute detail, while also requiring the teacher to be flexible enough to accommodate matters arising from class discussions, new lines of enquiry to follow and opportunities to address misconceptions and any lack of understanding that might become apparent during the lesson.

Short-term plans also need to be able to accommodate the children's learning speed. In the course of a scheme of work, the children may not complete tasks or grasp understanding in a particular area at the same time; therefore, lessons need to be able to stimulate all learners and be pitched correctly for a range of skills, knowledge and abilities. Cooper (2012: 86) reminds us that 'it is essential that the learning objectives are simple, manageable, attainable, realistic and time-related (SMART)'. In terms of our history teaching, we also need to ensure that learning objectives are focused upon the historical aspect of the lesson. This may seem obvious, but lessons need to be aligned in order for them to be as effective as possible. Alignment sees the objective in line with the activity and the assessment or success criteria for the lesson. For instance, a learning objective for a historical aspect during a chronology topic that has addressed life in Tudor times may be 'to know the sequence of the wives of Henry VIII' or 'to correctly sequence, in chronological order, the wives of Henry VIII'. In order for the children to achieve the learning objective the activity will require the children to be engaged with sorting information or portraits of the six wives. This is a distinction between addressing the historical knowledge and understanding and historical skills that you might want to address. The teacher can control the amount of detail that is shared and the information with which the children will be discussing the order of the wives. The ability to move physical objects representing the wives is useful here in order to instigate discussion among the children. The objects used here could range from portraits of the wives to talk buttons with prepared biographies of each wife. The middle stage of alignment is monitoring that the children have achieved the learning objective. This might take the form of a set of success criteria for the lesson, written sentences in an exercise book, a photograph of the sequence the children have created or a physical timeline using the portraits or talk buttons.

Marking is, in some form, the final stage of alignment. Here, the children find out whether they have completed the task successfully or not. This might be conducted as part of a plenary to a lesson or, more formally, a marked piece of work. If the marking feeds back on the use of capital letters and full stops and does not address the sequencing of the six wives or acknowledge the rationalising that has taken place in order for the children to arrive at their final sequence, then the process is not aligned. A child's work needs to be marked against the original objective. Detailed plans at this stage provide an opportunity for you to ensure that curriculum areas are covered effectively; this may well be part of the medium-term plans also, as indicated earlier, but needs to be reaffirmed here. Similarly, should the lesson be part of a cross-curricular or topic-based approach, then acknowledgement of the national curriculum for all the curriculum areas needs to be explicit at this stage of the planning. The learning objectives need to be outlined here, as do the details of activities the children will be engaged in. This will cover a range of areas, such as resources, individual children's needs, groupings and differentiation. Differentiation includes many aspects of learning, and each individual teacher will know the best way to help the children in their class to access the learning. This may be through additional support, resources, time, or tasks. It may consider the needs of individual children, such as their social and emotional needs or physical needs. Differentiation at the planning stage may also address other aspects of teaching and learning, such as behaviour, special educational needs/disability, English as an additional language, and areas of inclusion.

Detailed short-term plans provide an opportunity to indicate how an activity will be structured; this may include groups, which may be based upon attainment or friendship. Considering how sources will be shared, used and analysed will be part of a detailed short-term plan, as will success criteria, key vocabulary, the allocation of support staff in the classroom and plenary activities.

As identified earlier, schools will approach medium- and short-term plans differently. In the course of writing this book I spoke to many teachers who all provided similar, but contrasting, views as to the level of detail contained within their plans. This is similar to my own experiences as a teacher, where different heads would require different levels of detail in the weekly plans.

In our plans, school policy will likely determine whether or not homework is to be provided for history. If this is the case, you need to consider why you are setting homework. In short, what is the point? This might lead to a wider debate about the purpose of homework, but if homework is set at your school, then the purpose of the homework needs to be clear. Is it to consolidate understanding of lesson content or to introduce the next step in the children's learning in the scheme of work? Either way, homework that is set needs to be purposeful. It can be seen as being an additional chore; however, it can also be seen as a further opportunity to differentiate learning for the pupils in your class. It can be used as a form of baselining, continuous assessment or as an ongoing enquiry project. While not everyone agrees about setting homework, it can be motivating and can reinforce and impact upon other aspects of school life, such as behaviour and motivation, as well as strengthen the home–school link.

For you as the teacher, planning is not only the structure of activities to be implemented during the scheme of work, but also a clearly set-out plan of the intended progression for pupils. Using the skills progression table in Table 4.1, you can identify the stage or step where individual children are in your class and then identify appropriate next steps to progress their historical knowledge and understanding.

The skills table is designed in such a way that you can develop and adjust the steps to suit the needs of your class more fully. No single document can hope to completely categorise activities, skills, attributes and understanding for each and every school. Rather the opportunity exists to use this document as a basis for progression, giving you the potential to add to each step – using medium-term plans as guidance – in order to produce a bespoke document for your class and, in the case of the history coordinator, the school as a whole. This document then can be used to monitor progression by class, or for each individual child.

The history coordinator

The history coordinator, or foundation subject manager in some schools, holds a really important post. With much of the attention within primary education being focused on maths and English, subjects such as history can sometimes be considered a poor relation in the curriculum, certainly in terms of prestige, finance and time. However, as we have already seen, a large proportion of teachers say that history is their favourite subject to teach and one of the most enjoyable in the curriculum. From this starting point, coordinators need to galvanise their staff and ensure that history is valued and taught well across the school. Some will take this further and will create or belong to a cluster group of schools with a curriculum interest in history. This may entail regular network meetings, twilights, joint continued professional development and in-service training days, as well as consultation with university partners, subject leads, authority personnel and education officers from heritage sites and museums. Talking points may include planning, approaches to teaching, joint ventures, local opportunities, forthcoming anniversaries and notable dates both locally and nationally, and a sharing of resources, experiences and a general developing of a collegiate working relationship. Many colleagues, especially those new to their role, will find such collaboration useful. Providing a collegiate atmosphere for good practice to develop and be shared is a valuable and worthwhile use of our time, as nurturing interest and a considered and rigorous approach to the teaching of history is of great importance. At such meetings, links can be forged, contacts made and experiences shared. One particular way in which this may manifest itself is with the sharing of resources. In order to provide artefacts for lessons, schools require big budgets and lots of storage space, which may not always be available. Through network meetings and cluster groups of schools, this particular hurdle may be overcome.

Planning for purposeful learning experiences may incorporate any number of approaches to teaching history. Enquiry has been put forward as a key foundation of teaching history; therefore, planning for enquiry is essential in order to embed this approach into our practice.

Planning for a research, or enquiry, project requires the children to develop a number of skills and concepts. You will need to consider how this enquiry will be structured. For instance, the investigation could be prompted by a question: what was it like to be a 10-year-old in Skara Brae? Or an enquiry might be triggered by an artefact or a mystery object, such as the pastry cutter in Figure 3.2. In turn this could lead to work about domestic life in each period, which could then lead to other areas of life being investigated and explored. Similarly, an enquiry around ancient Greece could be inspired by the object in Figure 6.1.

As we have already seen, questioning is integral to enquiry, and the skill of questioning needs to be practised and developed. Hoodless (2008) suggests that this questioning needs to be modelled by the teacher in order for the children to learn to ask purposeful questions and then to be able to proceed with their investigation. The children need to make notes of their questions and responses and thoughts; this will help them sift through their thoughts at a later stage and arrive at their final conclusions. They may also note that there is more than one feasible response or conclusion and that further investigation is needed. Guiding the children towards simple what, when, where, who, how and why questions will also focus thinking and open the door for work involving interpretation, reliability of evidence and their ability to 'sift arguments' and 'weigh evidence' (DfE, 2013).

The children may need time to process their own understanding as they tackle the process aspect of history in their work. This links to the preferred learning style of individual children. Gardner's work (1993, 2006) is much followed and informs us of

Figure 6.1 Ancient Greek discus

dominant styles of learning. We can see that for ourselves, in our own preferred ways of working (e.g. a quiet room, a silent section of the library, or with the TV or radio on in the background). We will also be aware that at different times and in learning different things, different approaches will work. You might follow a recipe from a book in order to learn how to cook a particular dish, but you are unlikely to learn how to drive from a book. You might learn a new chord on the guitar by being shown rather than from reading where to put your fingers. The same can be said for the children we teach; they each come with their own preferences, tolerances and intolerances towards lessons, school, their teacher and the content, as well as an 'individual' preference as to how they want to be taught on any given day. This might lead you to consider how activities are structured and delivered, either by table or friendship groups, pairs or individual work. Decisions made here will affect how work is presented, shared and communicated.

Planning at Key Stage 1 involves consideration of how you want to present opportunities to engage in historical thinking to their classes. In many cases opportunities will involve not only curriculum-based work but also activities that are directly related to developing specific aspects of historical understanding, for instance a sequencing activity. Sequencing is a skill that helps develop good chronological understanding. At Key Stage 1 there are opportunities to sequence events in a familiar story as an aspect of historical work. For instance, working with traditional tales allows you to split the story into sections, with each section flowing into the next. A sequential story, such as the 'Three Little Pigs', is ideal as the children will be familiar with the order of events in the tale and will be able to rearrange, sort and sequence flash cards depicting the events in the story, into the right order. Other traditional tales, such as 'Red Riding Hood' or 'Goldilocks and the Three Bears' would work similarly well. Equally, Michael Rosen's *We're Going on a Bear Hunt* (1993) is structured in such a way that sequencing the events allows the children to retell the story, check accuracy and agree upon their final sequence.

For older children, the rooms visited at Willy Wonka's factory in Roald Dahl's *Charlie and the Chocolate Factory* (1964) or the order in which the children disappear allows for the same engagement with sequencing and chronology.

At Key Stage 1, the children are likely to encounter historical ideas through nursery rhymes, children's stories and traditional tales. These links to the past are important in developing and understanding the world and are an important opportunity to begin to address aspects of history, such as change, through such sources. Books such as the Paddington Bear stories arguably refer to an England of a bygone time. Modern adaptations in film may update the Paddington stories, but the original texts allude to a simpler time before mobile phones and social media and tablets filled our lives. Similarly, stories such as Enid Blyton's Famous Five series describe an idyllic version of school holidays that offered a freedom and adventure unlike anything that most children today would recognise. Of course, texts such as the Famous Five are more suited to older children in Key Stage 2 as, in addition to the historical content that can be drawn upon in lessons, there are opportunities to discuss change in terms of society's attitudes and values, as well as some of the liberties that Julian, Dick, George, Anne and Timmy the dog enjoyed.

Planning at Key Stage 1 can also develop historical understanding through vocabulary. The terms used and modelled by you as the teacher are important here in consolidating understanding and confidence among children to use the correct terms and phrases for themselves. Since modelling the correct use of vocabulary is good practice, ensuring that opportunities arise within lessons in order to consolidate understanding is essential. So, too, is making good use of children's prior knowledge and experiences. For instance, everyday experiences, such as birthdays, seasons, days of the week and even the school timetable, all present opportunities to work with sequencing and chronology. At Key Stage 1, other aspects of history can be addressed through story, as well as other sources of information. The use of story is advocated by Bage (2002) and is a widely used approach in classrooms as children explore the past. Chronicling the past can involve oral history; this may take place within a local study unit and may highlight change in the local area. This is likely to be supported with other forms of evidence such as maps and photographs. Similar work, investigating personal histories and adopting the idea of Cooper's 'Me' topic (Cooper 2012: 100), could take place at Key Stage 1 in order to develop a sense of the past as well as a sense of identity and belonging.

Younger children may explore the past through themes and topics. The national curriculum at Key Stage 1 (DfE, 2013) requires the children to look at specific areas in history, such as comparing the first flight with space exploration. The opportunities here for you to develop work in the area of exploration and flight are endless, with potential visits to airfields, airports and aviation museums, such as the Royal Air Force Museum in Cosford, Shropshire. This will provide opportunities for the children to compare materials, safety and use.

Approaches to teaching younger children may also include opportunities for historical play. As with any approach to teaching and learning, play needs to be planned. This may seem like a contradiction to the idea of play itself but makes sense in the context of planning opportunities for the children to engage in historical ideas and understanding and take ownership of the activities themselves. Such activities can be enhanced through adult-led play that promotes social interaction and discovery about the world. Discussion about the play that has occurred can help establish and then consolidate links to the past, early engagement with aspects of history, such as change, and the further development of historical knowledge and understanding.

At this early stage of children's learning, creating opportunities to think historically is of immense importance. The children you teach may well be the historians of the future, and it may well be the contact with historical activities that they experience in your class that sets them on that path.

Key Stage 1 children can explore chronology through interactive timelines, perhaps using pegs and washing lines, talking pegs or items laid on a table. These may form part of a display that can be used during lessons, providing children with the opportunity to sequence photographs, clothes, toys and their own pictures of memories or written accounts. Such planned activities need a clear historical learning objective and need to be part of a structured, considered learning experience.

Planning at Key Stage 2 can incorporate opportunities to address the content and process of history. Here, children can be engaged in activities that require them not only to develop their subject knowledge in terms of the dates and events of the past but also to engage more critically with concepts, attitudes and values. They will have started this journey during their Key Stage 1 work, but at Key Stage 2 it needs developing further.

Therefore, we would expect planned activities for children to question evidence, inter-rogate sources and provide justification for decisions and thoughts about the past that includes reasoned arguments and an understanding of empathy. As we have seen ear-lier in this book, history itself is a lot more involved that simply regurgitating the sto-ries of the past. Children need to be engaged in the process of history in order to fully appreciate the stories of the past. Therefore, as a teacher of primary history you need to design, plan and implement learning experiences that provide opportunities for the children to develop all facets of their historical understanding.

Enquiry, of course, will loom large in many teachers' history planning. As we have seen, initial enquiries may stem from the children's own curiosity, a misconception you want to address or a predetermined line of enquiry that you have identified and planned for. Within the classroom, you can look to provide opportunities to use a wide range of artefacts and sources in order to create meaningful lessons and inspire the children in the class.

In recent years, learning outside the classroom (Department for Education and Skills (DfES), 2006) has increased dramatically in significance, with many teachers advocating such experiences as being beneficial not just to the child and their learning in history but also through development in several other key areas. The Council for Learning Outside the Classroom states that 'every young person [0–19 years] should experience the world beyond the classroom' (DfES, 2006). It claims that among the ben-efits of LOtC are raised attainment, reduced truancy and an awareness of 'the wonders of areas such as art, heritage, culture, adventure and the natural world'. It promotes any learning that takes place outdoors, including the school grounds, as well as other areas of the curriculum. That said, a trip during a scheme of work often lends itself to a visit to a museum, gallery or site associated with the topics covered in history.

Any learning that takes place outside the classroom requires thorough planning. Planning a school trip can be a fraught experience, involving the logistics of the day, the cost, and organising an army of volunteer helpers. There are practical considera-tions, such as medications (e.g. inhalers), lunch provision, and you will likely develop an unhealthy obsession with the weather forecast for the day in addition to the teaching and learning activities that the children will engage with once they are there. However, despite these factors, a well-planned school trip is a rewarding experience.

There are a number of areas to consider in order to provide a valuable experience for the children. Firstly, where will you go? This should not be determined by the prox-imity of the site, but by the educational value of the visit. Preferably, it is an opportunity to experience something that cannot be addressed in the classroom. Secondly, when will you go? This may be determined by the availability of the venue when you book it, but pedagogical considerations should also be taken into account here. Do you want the trip to inspire the rest of the scheme of work, or do you want the children to have a solid knowledge base before the trip itself? There is no real right or wrong here; this can only be decided by the teacher and the needs of the class. Another consideration involves the activities the children will be engaged with once they are at the venue. Will these be led by staff at the museum, you or another adult? All the staff need to be familiar with the aims of the trip in order to help you and your class make the most of the visit. The day needs to be carefully structured. Carousel groups can work well, with the assigned expert adult repeating activities with different groups throughout the day, whether that is the teacher or a member of the education team at the site.

Not all learning outside the classroom needs to take place at a specific venue. The idea of a 'micro' learning outside the classroom activity can lead to interesting opportunities by just using the immediate environment – the school grounds and within the school building. For an effective learning journey I would suggest following a three-step structure. Promoted by Beames and Ross (2010) as outdoor journeys, learning journeys can be used to help the children note their surroundings and ask questions about their immediate environment. The three steps see the children move from question to research to communication, and can be developed with children of any age. A learning journey can be used by the children to generate questions, based upon what they have seen and noted while on their walk. These questions can be used as a line of enquiry in future lessons. The structure of a learning journey can be applied to any area within the curriculum, and they are useful in helping to recognise that history is all around us and centres around everyday lives, weaving throughout times past. It is an important cognitive step for the children to take in their historical development.

You may choose to structure a learning journey to highlight specific things, such as date stones, commemorative plaques and cups in the school trophy cabinet (should the walk include inside the school as well as outside). Some schools mark occasions of local or national significance with plaques and inscriptions, while past teachers may donate books, sculptures or similar objects to the school creating more date-specific resources in and around the building with which the children can work. Similarly, benches, trees and flower beds within the school grounds that have particular significance may also hold clues about the past of the school and its community. Inside, schools may display photographs of the school and its former pupils through the decades, with some photographs having particular relevance to some of the contemporary children as their parents may be past pupils and can be seen during their school days. These examples can all be used to address aspects of history and, of course, the premise of a learning journey can be expanded outside the school grounds and applied to the immediate local area where street signs, pub names and architectural features will raise questions about the past for the children.

We have talked about historical learning objectives and recognised that the wording of these objectives informs whether the objective is concerned with a historical skill, i.e. to be able to, or a historical concept, i.e. to understand our knowledge and to know. Of course, other objectives exist such as those designed to recap information and consolidate understanding. However, most objectives will fall into these two categories. This helps keep lesson planning focused, as lessons should be driven by the objective and not the activity. Therefore, you will know that your pupils have covered a range of concepts and skills through careful planning rather than planning a lesson around an end product or an activity found online. The real art of teaching comes down to these finer points.

You will also need to consider the aims of the national curriculum and the purpose of study outlined within the document. Some of the statements and phrases that appear in the purpose of study for the history curriculum we have already considered, such as 'inspire pupils' curiosity', 'the process of change', 'ask perceptive questions, think critically, weigh evidence' and 'sift arguments'. Other aspects of the purpose of study provide further areas to plan for and explore, such as 'examining the complexity of people's lives' and 'the diversity of societies and relationships between different groups'. Planning to address these areas will require you to provide a range of evidence around a subject in order for the children to explore in the intended detail indicated here. Similarly, contrasting views need to be provided in order to create a complete picture of a specific period of time. This can be a time-consuming exercise but wholly worthwhile.

Identity is also referred to directly within the purpose of study. Knowledge and understanding regarding one's own identity enhance learning and the predisposition of pupils towards their own learning. This, therefore, is of great importance to those of us concerned with the process of learning and the greater purpose of education in general. The fact that identity is highlighted as an aspect of the purpose of study suggests that you should explore and investigate ways in which our identity is formed and its impact on each individual as discussed in Chapter 5. This provides us with an opportunity to explore the themes and ideas of Bourdieu (1997) within our lessons and class discussions.

The aims of the primary history curriculum convey the rhetoric we explored in Chapter 1, with children required to 'know and understand the history of these islands as a coherent, chronological narrative'. The aims also talk of 'this nation' and 'how Britain has influenced and been influenced by the wider world'. While some statements appear to refer to curriculum areas, such as ancient civilisations and non-European societies, some phrases appear to be open to interpretation. One such example is 'the follies of mankind'. To some people, this may appear to refer to war; however, it could also be applied to other aspects of the past, such as policies of governments in the past, or more contemporary issues such as the threat of terrorism in the twenty-first century. The curriculum, we should remind ourselves, is a bare minimum of content, and other topics and areas of interest can be discussed and addressed across the school year in addition to the content of the primary history curriculum.

An interesting aspect of the aims of the curriculum is the reference to 'abstract terms'. Examples provided include 'empire', 'civilisation', 'parliament' and 'peasantry'. As these are only suggestions, teachers are at liberty to add their own abstract terms, for example, settlement, policy, national identity, jingoism, nationalism and imperialism.

As we have seen, historical concepts are covered within the aims of the curriculum, highlighting the importance of both the content and process of history within our teaching. Children are encouraged to 'make connections, draw contrasts, analyse trends, frame historically valid questions and create their own structured accounts'. In order for the children to achieve this they need to experience structured learning experiences that provide opportunities in these areas. If the children are, for example, to draw contrasts, then they at least need to access contrasting accounts. Opportunities such as these, of course, need effective planning. You will want to provide such opportunities throughout their history lessons during the children's time in Key Stages 1 and 2 in order to build upon and consolidate knowledge and understanding.

The aims of the curriculum also present opportunities to consider knowledge within different contexts as well as emphasising the importance of enquiry and evidence in the children's learning of history.

At university we discuss aspects of history teaching that we might see in a good, well-balanced history lesson. Using a prompt sheet that we will explore in more detail in Chapter 8, trainee teachers try to ensure that they provide coverage of a range of activities and experiences within their lessons.

Summary

In this chapter, planning has become the focus of our thoughts as we have explored how the teaching and learning that we aspire to can be created and implemented in the classroom. The importance of structured learning experiences has been emphasised, along with the wide range of opportunities that we seek to include in our schemes of work. We have considered both key stages and linked our thinking about history teaching to the approaches we adopt for the different needs of our children.

References

Bage, G. (2002) *Narrative Matters: Teaching and Learning History through Story*. London. Falmer Press.

Beames, S. and Ross, H. (2010) Journeys outside the classroom. *Journal of Adventure Education & Outdoor Learning* 10(2): 95–109.

Bourdieu, P. (1997) *The Love of Art* (new edition). Oxford: Polity Press.

Cooper, H. (2012) *History 5–11: A Guide for Teachers*. Abingdon: Routledge.

Dahl, R. (1964) *Charlie and the Chocolate Factory*. New York: Alfred A. Knopf.

Department for Education (2013) *The National Curriculum for England*. London: DfE.

Department for Education and Skills (2006) *Learning Outside the Classroom Manifesto*. Nottingham: DfES.

Gardner, H. (1993) *Frames of Mind: The Theory of Multiple Intelligences*. London: Fontana.

Gardner, H. (2006) *Multiple Intelligences: New Horizons in Theory and Practice*. New York: Basic Books.

Hoodless, P. (2008) *Teaching History in Primary Schools*. Exeter: Learning Matters.

Jones, M. (2011) What history should we teach? The teachers' perspective: The Historical Association's Primary Survey. *Primary History* 57.

Kolb, D.A. (1984) *Experiential Learning: Experience as the Source of Learning and Development*. Englewood Cliffs, NJ: Prentice Hall.

Maddison M, (2014) The National Curriculum for History from September 2014: The view from Ofsted. *Primary History* 66.

Ofsted (2011) *History for All*. London: Ofsted,

Reynolds, A. and Hodkinson, A. (2011) How to teach chronology. *Primary History* 57.

Rosen, M. (1993) *We're Going on a Bear Hunt*. London. Walker.

7

Assessment

This chapter explores assessment in primary history and the challenges of assessment in the primary classroom. We highlight opportunities for assessment within the history lessons that we plan, while considering what we are assessing in terms of the content and process of history and how it is to be assessed. This chapter also considers current guidance regarding assessment without levels and how this will impact upon teachers in the classroom.

Policies and practices regarding assessment vary from school to school; given that assessment itself means different things to different people, this means that talking about assessment can be a minefield. For our purposes, assessment here refers to the monitoring of the children's knowledge and understanding of history in the lessons they have and the topics they have covered.

In Chapter 6, we acknowledged how assessment opportunities need to be incorporated into the planning stage. This means that careful consideration as to what will be assessed has already been thought about by the class teacher. A danger at this stage is that the lesson becomes driven by the end product, whether that be a poster, a piece of work, a podcast or a presentation. This can mean that the integrity of the intended historical objectives of the lesson become lost or swept up by the importance placed upon the completion of the task and the end product. The children can also become focused on the end product rather than the intended learning. This is not the only potential pitfall when it comes to considering assessment of our history units. The Historical Association provides a useful resource that highlights key principles of assessment in primary history. Lomas (2014) writes that assessment needs to be manageable in terms of the amount of data collected. Too much, he warns, renders the system pointless. Another consideration is that the form of assessment that is chosen conforms to the whole-school policy implemented across all subjects in the school. Lomas (2014) consolidates our earlier observation that assessment opportunities should be considered at the planning stage. The concept of alignment is alluded to as well, in which the children will be assessed against the learning objectives and, if relevant, clearly defined success criteria.

Assessment should make good use of a range of approaches, with both formal and informal assessment taking place. Not all will agree with this sentiment, especially concerning formal tests; however, I find that quizzes can be used effectively and, if presented well, can provide motivation for the children as they enjoy competing with their peers. Quizzes can also be used both to impart information during lessons and as a form of assessment. Some activities or settings, of course, will not lend themselves so much to that kind of assessment. In these cases, alternative approaches can be used; these can be as straightforward as asking questions to garner the level of understanding among individuals in the class, or using observation, or discussing the findings or the activity the children have engaged with. Of course, marking work will also form part of the assessment process and allows the teacher to provide individual feedback to each child. Although time-consuming, marking is another aspect of a teacher's workload that can be seen as highly important, as feedback often creates and builds good relationships with the children as they value the comments you leave in their work. Marking fosters confidence and motivation among the children, and supportive comments at the end of work let the children know their work has been not only read and marked but also appreciated. Comments, therefore, enhance the pupil–teacher relationship, which in turn can have a positive impact in other areas of school life.

Lomas (2014) highlights the importance of a simple recording system, which provides an indication of each child's progress 'at a glance'. To many, a simple 'traffic light' system or a manageable symbol system will suffice to indicate a child's attainment. Again, it is likely that such a system will be in place for all curriculum subjects and will follow a whole-school policy, in order to ensure consistency for the teaching staff. For history, an important consideration is that the assessment covers a range of the aspects of history that we have looked at in this book. The skills progression table in Chapter 4 (Table 4.1) can provide some structure for such an exercise, as would Byrom (2014). Similar progression tables can be found online and can be seen as an initial response to the idea of assessing without levels. The 2014 national curriculum (DfE, 2013) removed levels, leaving schools with no clear way forward. Levels were first introduced in 1988 (Brill and Twist, 2013) and had provided a structure for monitoring progress that teachers had grown used to. However, levels were not universally appreciated and it would be easy to say that they were not particularly fit for purpose. They were seen as too subjective and open to interpretation by individual teachers. They did not allow for subtleties in knowledge and understanding and could be seen as influencing plans in order for children to climb up the scale. So, in this light, change and the removal of levels should be seen as a good thing. Resources such as the skills progression table here and Byrom (2014) should not be regarded as rewriting levels; these resources and others like them have been created in order to ensure coverage and progression is maintained in our schools in the absence of levels. There is much good practice taking place in our schools, and this needs to be preserved and maintained.

The Commission on Assessment without Levels (McIntosh, 2015) aims to provide guidance for schools. It states that the outputs of the Commission 'will set out the various purposes of assessment to clarify for teachers and parents how assessment without levels supports teaching and learning, and will develop principles which will support schools in developing effective systems of assessment which both contribute to and measure pupil progress and attainment in ways that assessment with levels failed to do' (McIntosh, 2015).

A shift in culture is also needed. Teachers will always want to 'evidence' their judgements on attainment, as that is what they have been trained to do, whereas effective assessment may not always produce a tangible end product. Schools will also be aware that if they are deemed to be 'coasting' then they might lose their quality status and be forced down the academy route. This, it could be argued, would indicate more of a need to evidence progression. However, Ofsted (2015) states that: 'When considering the school's records for progress of current pupils, inspectors will recognize that schools are at different points in their move towards adopting a system of assessment without national curriculum levels.'

In addition, 'Ofsted does not expect to see any specific frequency, type or volume of marking and feedback; these are for the school to decide through its assessment policy'. This seems to be neither comforting nor reassuring as schools, coordinators and school managers are still left with no real guidance. In addition, there is an implicit understanding that this arrangement is temporary and that uncertainty created here will also add to the pressure surrounding assessment. While we wait to see how the Commission resolves this state of affairs, we can look at the baselines for assessment. As asserted earlier, for our purposes, we are considering assessment to be the monitoring of children's knowledge and understanding of history and their progression in the subject.

Firstly, we need to know who we are assessing for. Secondly, what we are assessing. Thirdly, how will we assess? Finally, what do we do with that information? Let us take each point in turn, bearing in mind that the goalposts will doubtless move again.

Who are we assessing for?

Assessing foundation subjects may appear to carry less significance than assessing core subjects. However, providing feedback to parents about their child's progress is an important part of the teaching and learning cycle, especially as some children will flourish in subjects other that those deemed to be 'core'. Similarly, as a class teacher you will need to be accountable to your head teacher as to the progress the children are making in your class. Perhaps most importantly of all, the children themselves appreciate knowing how well they are working and will appreciate some feedback about their work. Of course, within the realm of assessment, different types of assessment are referred to. For the head teacher, the most useful data will be class records indicating the progress of all the children. While this kind of information might be interesting to parents, they, like the children themselves, are probably more concerned with the day-to-day attainment of their child.

Another reason why we assess, is of course, for yourself. As a conscientious practitioner, you will want to evaluate your teaching in order to inform your future plans and allow you to make adjustments and address misconceptions. You will also annotate plans in order to remind yourself to revisit sections in order to ensure understanding across your class.

What are we assessing?

As we have discovered, history in the past was traditionally seen as being concerned with facts, dates and significant people and events. As Hoodless (2008) points out, this is perhaps the easiest aspect of history to assess. Subject knowledge is an important part of what history is and can easily be tested. However, as we also know, this is not the only aspect of history and neither is this kind of assessment a true picture of knowledge and understanding. For assessment to be meaningful, both the content and process of history need to be assessed. For you as a teacher and for history coordinators, this requires an approach that will measure children's understanding of historical skills and concepts. Possibilities present themselves for using statements in the purpose of study and aims (see Table 7.1). By using the statements within the national curriculum document as a structure for assessing the children's progress in these areas, you can be confident that you are monitoring the children's knowledge and understanding of history in a purposeful and meaningful way that goes over and above just monitoring subject knowledge.

Table 7.1 National curriculum for history: purpose and aims

Purpose of Study

A high-quality history education will help pupils gain a coherent knowledge and understanding of Britain's past and that of the wider world. It should inspire pupils' curiosity to know more about the past. Teaching should equip pupils to ask perceptive questions, think critically, weigh evidence, sift arguments, and develop perspective and judgement. History helps pupils to understand the complexity of people's lives, the process of change, the diversity of societies and relationships between different groups, as well as their own identity and the challenges of their time. (DfE, 2013)

Aims

The national curriculum for history aims to ensure that all pupils:
- know and understand the history of these islands as a coherent, chronological narrative, from the earliest times to the present day: how people's lives have shaped this nation and how Britain has influenced and been influenced by the wider world
- know and understand significant aspects of the history of the wider world: the nature of ancient civilisations; the expansion and dissolution of empires; characteristic features of past non-European societies; achievements and follies of mankind
- gain and deploy a historically grounded understanding of abstract terms such as 'empire', 'civilisation', 'parliament' and 'peasantry'
- understand historical concepts such as continuity and change, cause and consequence, similarity, difference and significance, and use them to make connections, draw contrasts, analyse trends, frame historically-valid questions and create their own structured accounts, including written narratives and analyses
- understand the methods of historical enquiry, including how evidence is used rigorously to make historical claims, and discern how and why contrasting arguments and interpretations of the past have been constructed
- gain historical perspective by placing their growing knowledge into different contexts, understanding the connections between local, regional, national and international history; between cultural, economic, military, political, religious and social history; and between short- and long-term timescales. (DfE, 2013)

In following this approach, assessment of some historical concepts will be developed. You may feel that these statements could be adapted to ensure coverage of other concepts within the sphere of primary history. In addition, good practice in assessing history will involve the use of a wide range of judgements in all areas of history, in order to ensure that assessment is fair and meaningful.

How are we going to assess?

Assessment is often broken down into two different categories: formative assessment and summative assessment. These are the kinds of assessment that you most frequently see taking place in schools.

Summative assessment is a 'summary' of a child's attainment. This may be a mark for a test or a percentage grade. Summative assessment is usually used to provide an indication of where a child is at in terms of their progression. It will inform reports to parents, parents' evening conversations as well as providing the 'meat' for data analysis of school managers, outside agencies and, of course, Ofsted. In recent times, much emphasis has been placed on such assessment for the school.

Formative assessment 'informs' the child as to what to do next in order to improve their work. This concerns itself with feedback and target setting in order to focus a child's attention on the next step. Formative assessment can take place in various forms, such as a question during a lesson that prompts a child's thinking, or a discussion about work with an evaluative slant that is designed to help a child see mistakes or misconceptions in their own work.

What are we going to do with the assessment?

The purpose of collecting assessment data is to improve and inform the practice of teaching in the class. On an individual level children benefit from feedback and support and the guidance offered through assessment. This is especially the case if the process of assessment is seen as a positive aspect of lessons rather than a formal and intimidating experience that is to be endured. For schools, assessment is essential part of school life, as much of the status, funding and reputation of the school, both in education circles and locally, is derived from the perceived attainment of the school and their shared results.

When considering assessment, links can be made to learning theories. We have already considered Kolb (1984) in our previous chapter on planning. We can also consider assessment in light of Vygotsky's (1978) zone of proximal development, whereby such conversations and discussions, led by an expert or 'capable other', can lead learners into new fields of knowledge and understanding. Similarly, Bloom's taxonomy (Bloom et al., 1956) can also be seen as a useful model for teachers as, by using the model, teachers not only plan activities of increasing challenge but also can assess understanding in terms of children's attainment within the hierarchy of the model. This may not mean a guaranteed attainment and full understanding, but it does provide an indication.

In addition to more traditional methods of assessment such as tests, assessment can include any number of forms. Observation itself can be used by teachers in order to assess how well a child (or a group of children) addresses a task, as well as providing information on how well they work with others and how long they stay on task. Hoodless (2008) points out that, while observing, teachers are at liberty to write 'field notes' in order to refer back to at a later date. Another form of assessment, already alluded to, is discussion. Discussion cannot be underestimated as a form of assessment as it provides an informal setting in which a child can elaborate on their understanding of a particular topic and a safe environment that might highlight their limitations in terms of knowledge and understanding of the given topic. Both methods of assessment, observation and discussion, can provide information on children's subject knowledge and their understanding of the processes of history.

Informally, children can be quizzed regularly about their current topic of study and they can be encouraged to provide rationales and explanations for their thinking.

Self-assessment provides another insight into a child's own thinking about their learning. This may take the form of a sheet or 'comment card' that the children complete at the end of a lesson, or it could be considered as part of an overarching discussion. This may be held by table groups or as a whole-class plenary activity. There will always be a debate about how reliable such an approach can be, but sometimes using self-assessment, especially when measuring understanding of concepts rather than factual details, which could be assessed through other means, is a worthwhile exercise. Self-assessment also provides a sense of ownership and control for the child as to their learning in the topic. This can nurture confidence and self esteem.

Mind mapping is another reliable and informal means of assessment. Through mind mapping children have the opportunity to record their new found knowledge and understanding. A structured mind map, such as in Figure 7.1, allows teachers to prompt for information.

In contrast, an open mind map, such as in Figure 7.2, provides the opportunity for children to recall information and other details regarding the topic they are currently studying. This simple form of assessment can be revisited and added to as a topic progresses. You can use this to monitor progression and evidence 'value added' throughout the topic. The activity of completing the mind maps can also be incorporated into lessons either as introductions to lessons that begin with a recap of the previous learning in the scheme of work, or as an evaluative plenary activity.

Writing frames, as advocated by Lewis and Wray (1995), are also a superb means of recording children's levels of understanding as well as of addressing the quality and structure of non-fiction writing.

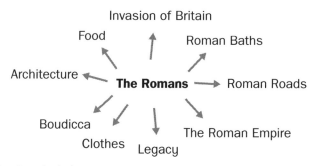

Figure 7.1 Structured mind map

Figure 7.2 Open mind map

In recent years, discussion about assessment of learning and assessment for learning has been superseded by the disappearance of levels for assessment and the impact
of such a move. However, it is important that, as practitioners new and old, we have an
understanding of these ideas that will influence our classroom practice. Assessment
of learning, as the term indicates, refers to summative methods of assessment, while
assessment *for* learning is concerned with formative assessment and the impact upon
future learning.

Table 7.2 highlights some of the ways in which we can incorporate assessment
opportunities into our history lessons. Methods such as outcomes and self-assessment
can themselves include any number of classroom ideas, such as coloured cards to indicate confidence for a typical self-assessment method and, of course, outcomes could
consist of anything ranging from written work in books to presentations. solutions to
problems or contributions to a discussion.

It is important to remember that any form of assessment is only ever a snapshot of
a particular moment in time. As your philosophy towards teaching forms, your thoughts
on assessment in particular and the who, how, and why of assessment will undergo a
number of changes. However, as a means of combating this 'snapshot' scenario, schools
are moving towards the idea of triangulation of assessment. Triangulation of assessment
is used in primary schools in order to gain a fair insight into a child's knowledge and
understanding and can therefore be used to monitor progress over time. Triangulation,
as the name suggests, requires teachers to form their assessments based upon three
inputs: tests, tasks and work. In this method, test results are compared with observations based upon children working on tasks where knowledge, skills and understanding
of a particular area are applied. This is then considered alongside final pieces of work
to provide a fairer picture of a child's overall level of attainment. This is an innovative
approach designed to provide a more rigorous and complete picture of a child's abilities
rather than a single snapshot that a single form of assessment may have provided.

Of course, any form of assessment will always provoke discussion. As we have
seen, it is far easier to assess subject knowledge in history but this would mean that
while the 'content' of history was being assessed, the 'process' was not. Therefore, we
need to devise methods of ensuring that skills and understanding are also assessed as

Table 7.2 Forms of Assessment

Formal Testing	Quiz	Observation	Discussion	Mind Mapping
Field Notes	Self-assessment	Writing frames	Outcomes	Think, pair, share

the children progress through the school. This in itself comes with a warning. One deputy head teacher commented that

> assessment of historical skills is only going to be of benefit if your long-term plan is sufficiently thought through so as to allow for those skills to be revisited and developed again over time.

The toolkit idea contained here is designed to address several aspects of history and could be used as a form of assessment in monitoring understanding.

Toolkit idea 7.1

Cartoon

Aspects: Knowledge and understanding, interpretation, communication and organisation

Encouraging children to create interesting outcomes in their work not only inspires them, but also inspires you and makes marking seem much less of a mundane sport. While working towards an end product should not be the driving force of the lesson, it can be motivating, and seeing the children share their new knowledge is arguably the best thing about teaching. The end product can be almost anything. One challenge I regularly set for my class was to create a cartoon strip based upon the topic they were studying. This gave the children the opportunity to plot out their text and pictures over the course of the storyboard, making sure that they were including the salient points.

There is, of course, the danger that the task may turn into an art lesson. This can easily be avoided by the use of a class discussion at the start of the activity and through the use of well-placed mini-plenaries throughout the lesson. This ensures that the children do not lose focus on the main objectives of the lesson and provides you with a piece of work that clearly demonstrates their understanding.

Figure 7.3 represents a Year 3 child's understanding of Boudicca's revolt and was the end product of a series of lessons based around the events leading up to the revolt and the revolt itself. The speech bubbles convey an understanding of the events, as does the sequencing of the events in the storyboard.

Summary

In this chapter, we have seen that assessment of historical skills, knowledge and understanding can be conducted in many ways. Children can communicate and share their levels of understanding in a range of ways, from traditional written outcomes to more

Figure 7.3 Boudicca cartoon

creative ideas including the use of technology that allows children to create podcasts, presentations and films. We have also considered assessment without levels and the new direction this will take in light of the Commission on Assessment without Levels. Although this may provide some uncertainty as to the requirements for Ofsted in the near future, we are aware that the essence of assessment will remain the same and that, for history, this will involve the careful planning and assessment of both the content and process of history.

References

Bloom, B.S., Engelhart, M.D., Furst, E.J., Hill, W.H. and Krathwohl, D.R. (1956) *Taxonomy of Educational Objectives: The Classification of Educational Goals. Handbook I: Cognitive Domain*. New York: Longmans, Green.

Brill, F. and Twist, L. (2013) *Where Have All the Levels Gone? The Importance of a Shared Understanding of Assessment at a Time of Major Policy Change*. Slough: NFER.

Byrom, J. (2014) *Progression in History under the 2014 National Curriculum. A Guide for Schools*. London: Historical Association.

Department for Education (2013) *The National Curriculum for England*. London: DfE.

Hoodless, P. (2008) *Teaching History in Primary Schools*. Exeter: Learning Matters.

Kolb, D.A. (1984) *Experiential Learning: Experience as the Source of Learning and Development*. Englewood Cliffs, NJ: Prentice Hall.

Lewis, M. and Wray, D. (1995) *Developing Children's Non-fiction Writing: Working with Writing Frames*. Leamington Spa: Scholastic.

Lomas, T. (2014) *Assessment in Primary History*. London: Historical Association.

McIntosh, J. (2015) *Final Report of the Commission on Assessment without Levels*. London: DfE. https://www.gov.uk/government/uploads/system/uploads/attachment_data/file/461534/Commission_report_.pdf (accessed 25 September 2015).

Ofsted (2015) *School Inspection Handbook*. Manchester: Ofsted.

Vygotsky, L.S. (1978) *Mind in Society*. Cambridge, MA: Harvard University Press.

8

Theory into practice

For trainee teachers, newly qualified teachers (NQTs) and indeed more experienced teachers, making sense of what history is and how it fits into the curriculum and the lessons we deliver is the ultimate goal. As we have seen, history is a set of components that includes consideration of historical skills, concepts, attitudes, planning and assessing as well as a fine balance between the content of history and the process of history in preparing our schemes of work. This chapter will explore the intricacies involved in putting theory into practice.

Our own stance and experience with history is one consideration that can serve as a starting point. This may include a reflection upon our engagement with the subject of history, our own experiences of history lessons and our predisposition towards the subject. If we consider the *Teachers' Standards* (DFE, 2013a) then we know that this starting point should not be a barrier towards effective teaching as we are duty bound to 'plan and teach well structured lessons' (p. 11). Teachers are also required to 'demonstrate good subject knowledge and curriculum knowledge' (p. 11). Therefore, you need some form of collating and measuring your prowess in these areas.

Table 8.1 helps you audit your historical skills, experiences and understanding and has been created in order to help measure your starting point. Within it, you are encouraged to reflect upon aspects of your own understanding in relation to the subject of history. There are six key areas under consideration; general, chronology, belonging and identity, interpretation, pedagogy and practical approaches. Within each section, you are asked to consider a number of points. For instance, in the general category, we consider the focus of the national curriculum as well as aspects of history, such as chronology, empathy and interpretation that form the curriculum itself. Other considerations in this regard discuss the range of sources used in historical investigations as well as the concept of 'evidence' itself.

At my university, we encourage trainees to engage with this resource and to build up a portfolio of evidence to support their engagement with the different aspects covered by it. For example, when evidencing engagement with the chronology section of the table, some trainees include a piece of reflective writing that considers the advantages of teaching the curriculum in chronological order. This refers back to the discussion in Chapter 2 and Davies and Redmond's (2005) assertion that teaching in chronological order consolidates an understanding of chronology. These are the kinds of thought processes we want to encourage and nurture. While collecting evidence, there are often opportunities for debate. For instance, when considering pedagogy, links can be made to other areas of study such as teaching studies modules and other curriculum areas, including other humanities. This helps develop a sense of the bigger picture in your teacher training, to make links to learning theories and to see theoretical approaches in practice. The nature of enquiry-led lessons, museum visits and other approaches to teaching history present strong links to constructivism and socio-constructivism. Other areas in Table 8.1 can be evidenced through photographs of children working or of children's work. Similarly, resources, lesson ideas and practical approaches can also be included as part of the evidence engagement.

One of the main advantages of using the table is that the focus is not specifically on subject knowledge. Therefore you really start to engage with the document effectively when you realise that history teaching in the primary school is much more than teaching facts about certain topics. A further example of this is that you consider belonging and identity as part of your historical understanding. This broaches the subject of a sense of self and can lead classroom work into the realms of citizenship, tolerance, social cohesion, understanding and empathy. Both specialists and non-specialists need to be aware of the opportunities history offers in order to take advantage of them.

Table 8.1 is intended to be used as an initial starting point for diagnosing your areas of strength and areas for development. In engaging with this process, it is intended that you will develop a stronger sense of your own engagement and understanding of the discipline of history and the subject of history in the primary classroom.

AUDIT OF SKILLS

	History	
	SKILL/EXPERIENCE/UNDERSTANDING	EVIDENCE
General	• I know that the national curriculum focuses on knowledge, skills and understanding, and that this is spilt into chronological understanding, events, people and changes in the past, historical interpretation and historical enquiry. • I understand that aspects of history such as chronology, empathy and interpretation are important to the essence of what history is about. • Children's historical awareness begins before school age and is developed and shaped throughout their lives. • Children have differing needs and capacities at different ages. • I can identify a range of resources to support historical understanding and classroom practice.	

Continued

AUDIT OF SKILLS   *Continued*

	History	
	SKILL/EXPERIENCE/UNDERSTANDING	*EVIDENCE*
	• Children will interact and engage with history and historical themes throughout their lives, and these interactions enrich their experiences of life in both aesthetic and psychological fields. • Historical understanding requires an understanding of historical themes such as cause and effect and bias. • Many aspects of history are abstract. • Evidence and providence is important in establishing historical facts or truths. • Peoples' perceptions of historical events and the people of the past can be predetermined by their experiences and background.	
Chronology	• Events in the past happen in sequence and often there is a relationship between them in terms of cause and effect. • Children find understanding chronology and a sense of the very distant past, in particular, difficult to comprehend.	
Belonging and Identity	• History provides an essential opportunity for children to develop their sense of belonging and identity. • Teachers need to provide opportunities to engage with history in a variety of ways. • History is all around us and impacts upon us in all areas of our lives. • In their history lessons children learn to appreciate other cultures and identities.	
Interpretation	• Interpreting the past involves thinking and reflecting upon attitudes, motivating factors and decisions that may contradict our own initial feelings. • Interpreting past events involves a critical engagement but avoids judging people and events of the past • Interpreting events from the past is central to the process of understanding the past and the decisions people have made. • Interpretation requires an acceptance of opposing views and differing opinions.	

Pedagogy	• Historical understanding can be taught using a range of different approaches, advocated by a range of writers. • Children's capacity for historical understanding is affected by their stage of development. • Evidence and the use of artefacts helps provide context, structure and meaning to learning experiences. • A historical narrative also provides context for historical understanding. • The teaching of history should include a range of sources and materials.
Practical Approaches	• I understand a range of methods to develop historical understanding while on professional practice. • I understand that the national curriculum requires a range of ways in which findings and historical understanding is presented. • I understand that people's perceptions of historical points of view may be determined by their own backgrounds and experiences and that this might impact upon their engagement and motivation to learn. • Ethical considerations need to be addressed in planning teaching and learning activities that children will engage with. • Popular culture relates to historical events and times through stories, games, pictures, poems, films, adverts, toys, TV and everyday sayings. • I can use technology and new technologies to research historical topics as well as presenting findings. • I know that history can be taught with a range of approaches.

To further develop our understanding of good history teaching, we also need to think about what is considered to be good practice. In their professional development materials Ofsted (2012), highlighted 'the characteristics of highly effective teaching' as follows:

- thorough planning focused on clear subject-specific learning outcomes
- opportunities for pupils to ask valid historical questions, find answers and present their work to their peers
- opportunities for pupils to collaborate in questioning historical evidence
- opportunities to use and evaluate artefacts and real historical evidence
- careful subject-specific assessment during lessons of the progress and understanding of all pupils.

- thoughtful cross-curricular links which ensure that historical understanding is nurtured through other opportunities.
- imaginative use of the internet and the interactive whiteboard to bring variety to lessons but also to gain access to a wealth of historical resources.
- a creative balance between teacher-directed learning and independent learning.
- sensitive teaching so that pupils understand the changing views of the past, how and why interpretations and representations change, why history matters and why what they are taught is worth knowing.

These characteristics came about as a result of the *History for All* report (Ofsted, 2011) and, although written before the curriculum changed in 2014, they still offer a clear insight into what is expected in the classroom and what is considered to be good practice.

Equal consideration is also given to how teachers can 'ensure the best learning in history'. The materials highlight that 'Particularly effective practice was characterised by teachers who not only had good subject knowledge but also good subject pedagogy, that is, a good understanding of how pupils learn in the subject' (Ofsted, 2012). This point emphasises the 'all round' nature of our historical knowledge and understanding that is required for effective classroom practice.

Ofsted (2012) goes on to say that the most effective subject pedagogy, which ensured high achievement in history, was shown by teachers whose approach focused on well-structured enquiry, embracing independent thinking and learning. This further consolidates the message that enquiry is at the heart of effective history teaching. Key areas to consider here regarding effective teaching of history are that children are challenged effectively, that their interest is piqued and maintained, that children should not be given the answers but should think independently in finding out about the past and, in so doing, should consider the implications of what they have found out in terms of assimilating new knowledge and considering how this changes our understanding of the past. Ofsted (2012) is keen to highlight the 'subject specific thinking' which it feels should be evident in history lessons and promoted through effective teaching, including reference to 'cross-curricular links', perhaps indicating some form of acknowledgement of approaches to teaching history that are evident in schools.

In order to ensure good practice, trainee teachers, NQTs and teachers need not only to be aware of the principles of good practice but also to have the skills and organisational prowess to monitor their own teaching in order to ensure that such good intentions are being upheld. To this end, lesson prompts are provided (see Table 8.2) to help you consider your own planning and teaching and, furthermore, to evaluate the content coverage in lessons or indeed over an entire scheme of work.

Lesson observations are a familiar part of the lives of the performance review of trainee teachers, NQTs and teachers, and so considering our teaching in this way is not an alien concept. It is not intended that every lesson will address every prompt, since that would be impossible, impractical and not good practice; rather it is intended that the prompts are addressed over the course of a scheme of work, so that you can be confident as to the extent of the coverage of your lessons. The prompts were referred to in Chapter 6, and one example of such a resource considers three main areas to focus upon: the lesson plan; teaching and learning; and reflection. In this way, the prompts can be used as a planning tool in preparing schemes of work and helping to organise opportunities for experience. They can help focus attention on the different teaching approaches that are used, the range of resources used in lessons and the outcomes that the children produce.

While considering the lesson plan, the prompts ensure that there is a tight focus upon the historical elements of the lesson with reference to the national curriculum for history. Focus is also held on the importance of enquiry as teachers using the prompts are asked to consider whether the objectives are enquiry-led. In previous chapters, we have considered the importance of enquiry as a teaching approach. Here, enquiry is considered the driving force behind good practice in the classroom. Other considerations at this stage concern wider classroom considerations such as effective differentiation, inclusion and assessment. It is important, as we discovered in Chapter 7, that children are assessed against the historical objectives of the lesson.

Moving on to think about the lesson itself, teachers are prompted to think about the focused content of their lessons. Having considered history to be centred around skills, concepts and attitudes and values, the prompts also ensure that the content of history (subject knowledge) and the process of history (finding out about the past) are considered. The prompts also focus the activities of the lesson, ensuring that there is a range of methods and experiences included in lessons. Another consideration is that of the purpose of study in the national curriculum and the aims of the curriculum (DfE, 2013b). This ensures that lessons do not become entirely fact-based and that deep learning experiences that develop an appreciation of enquiry are established within lessons and the schemes of work. This links to our discussion on the purpose of study and the aims as an assessment tool in Chapter 7. Historical vocabulary and abstract terms are included, as is a focus upon a holistic approach to learning with reference made to cultural, economic, military, political, religious and social aspects. Similarly, the importance of developing aspects of history that deal with identity and belonging are considered here too.

The final section allows trainee teachers, NQTs and teachers to reflect upon their teaching experiences. Here you are asked to consider next steps, both for yourself and for the children you are teaching. A success criterion for the lesson helps consider whether the children's understanding of history has been developed and in what particular areas has this been successful (e.g. in developing historical skills, concepts, or attitudes and values).

The prompts can only ever be guidance to help structure the teaching and learning experiences that you plan. Some areas, such as chronology, are only referred to as part of the concepts of history, which is a reflection of its current driving force in primary history. Interpretation is another concept that is so embedded that it need not be singled out exclusively.

Teachers' views of history

With such mechanisms in place to help teachers provide quality lessons, we should consider the views of those who are teaching history. The view of history, when discussing the subject with a number of colleagues at various stages in their career and with a wealth of experiences and roles, is extremely positive. History is recognised as being of particular importance in the curriculum as it provides opportunities for the children to

Table 8.2 Lesson prompts

Lesson Plan

Does the plan include objectives for the national curriculum for history?

Are the objectives enquiry-led?

Are key questions included within the plan?

Is differentiation and the inclusion of all pupils considered within the plan?

Does assessment consider the specific historical focus of the lesson and the initial objectives?

Are there opportunities for the children to apply and demonstrate their knowledge and understanding of history?

Teaching and Learning

Do children have a secure historical knowledge?

Is there evidence of historical skills, concepts and attitudes and values being developed within the lesson?

Is there evidence of the content of history and the process of history being developed within the lesson?

Do activities address aspects of the purpose of the national curriculum and the aims of the national curriculum?

Do activities develop an understanding of abstract terms, such as 'empire', 'civilisation', 'parliament' and 'peasantry'?

Does the lesson develop a keen understanding of historical concepts such as change and continuity, cause and consequence, similarity, difference and significance?

Do activities provide opportunities for the children to demonstrate the ability to make connections, draw contrasts, analyse trends, frame historically valid questions and create structured accounts, including written narratives and analyses?

Do activities demonstrate an understanding of methods of historical enquiry and provide opportunities for the children to explore how evidence is used rigorously to make historical claims?

Do activities develop an understanding of how interpretations of the past have been constructed?

Do activities provide opportunities for the children to understand the connections between cultural, economic, military, political, religious and social history?

Is there an appropriate balance of first- and second-hand experience as relevant to the learning outcomes?

Is the activity interesting, and does it include opportunities for high-order, creative thinking?

Does the trainee promote a balanced perspective on events? For example, not promoting bias or stereotypes.

Are a range of methods employed in order for the children to investigate the past? Are they used effectively?

Is technology, including the internet, used appropriately?

How is history taught? Is there a strong focus on enquiry-led learning?

Are individual children's responses monitored?

Do aspects of the lesson recap on previous knowledge and experiences?

Is there sufficient focus on learning about history, particularly when the lesson involves other curriculum subjects?
Is there evidence of a practical hands-on enquiry?
Are concepts of evidence and provenance discussed and explored?
Are opportunities to discuss opposing views, different perspectives, bias and propaganda provided where appropriate?
Are aspects of history dealing with identity and belonging discussed and explored?

Reflection

When reflecting upon their lesson, is the teacher aware of how to develop historical knowledge and skills?
How did the lesson develop historical skills, concepts and attitudes and values?
Are clear 'next steps' identified for both the children and their learning and for the teacher and their own professional development?
How has the lesson impacted upon the children's developing understanding of history?
Has the success criterion been met?

make links with their surroundings and environment and with perspectives of time and space. For younger children especially, this is particularly emphasised, with early links focusing upon making sense of the world and their part in it.

One NQT, Jennifer, commented on the sheer joy that teaching the subject can bring, especially when 'seeing the children's understanding of the world develop through history' and recognising that 'their world has been shaped through events of the past'. Jennifer also notes how her class became 'intrigued' by events of the past, which certainly links to the ideas that history 'should inspire pupils' curiosity to know more about the past' (DFE, 2013b).

These thoughts are echoed by Sam, a Year 6 teacher, who noted during a trip to their local city whilst studying the locality that the children had appreciated the 'more obscure facts' and that they had remembered the smallest details of information that were shared with them while on the trip. This again relates to the children's basic interest in the past and that intrigue seems so widespread across all ages of children and across both key stages. Of course this needs nurturing and fostering among the teachers and children alike, but from a teacher's point of view this innate curiosity that has been identified within the children is also addressed through the attitudes and values that we, as teachers, convey as well as those attitudes that we wish the children to possess.

Focusing upon the joys of teaching history, a deputy head teacher, Katie, commented that the best thing about teaching history is that 'it's fascinating' and that 'it's lovely to see the children understand the past and make links to today'. She referred to children 'understanding the world around them', which serves to emphasise the importance of context in our teaching. Another positive highlighted by Katie was the recognition that children appreciate changes over time and how aspects of the past affect us now. The joy this teacher has for teaching history is evident when she finishes by proclaiming that 'I love it when they get excited and tell you random facts they remember'.

'Facts' in relation to teaching history have been mentioned on more than one occasion, and perhaps this is a good point to consider that despite lots of attention and focus being given to the process of history, within our thoughts, plans and delivery of lessons, there is still a place for hard facts and subject knowledge within our lessons and particularly as a hook on which to hang all the other aspects of history that we know to be so important.

Laura, a history coordinator, suggests that the best part of teaching history is the ability to teach creatively. She also notes that practical, hands-on, enquiry-based approaches enthuse the children and make teaching the subject fun. This is a far cry from the now outdated view of history lessons being boring. The value of links to other subjects was highlighted by Laura and a number of other colleagues. This does not mean that the integrity of history as a stand-alone subject is lost, rather that teaching and learning experiences can be enhanced as a result of the ability and freedom to provide a valuable context for the work. Laura, in her role as history coordinator, also appreciates the opportunities to provide fresh links to the community, as well as opportunities for investigations, trips and oral history and, through aspects of identity and belonging, the opportunities to develop strong home–school links that benefit other areas of school life too, including that of behaviour.

Of course, with all these benefits, there must be a downside to teaching history. Given the range of experiences among those interviewed here, it was interesting to see that responses were, in the main, generic to all schools, areas and experiences. Jennifer, the NQT, responded that challenges to teaching history were the lack of resources, and particularly authentic resources, and also that planning experiences and then planning lessons was very time-consuming. This is a common theme and a point that was raised by Emma, a final-year trainee, as well as Katie, the deputy head teacher, who similarly noted that planning history was time-consuming. This point was made with particular focus on developing the subject knowledge of staff: 'researching the subject knowledge before planning a unit and blending that with skills' takes time. The main challenges identified by Katie are those of 'ensuring that history skills are taught and that it is not just knowledge, knowledge, knowledge'. She says: 'Subject knowledge, particularly for less familiar topics, such as the Mayans or a study of Baghdad c. AD 900, is problematic in terms of time and resources and with less familiar topics, making work relevant can be even more of a challenge, especially for those with fewer years of teaching experience.' This is a point picked up by Jennifer, who acknowledged that 'sometimes the children will get restless, particularly if they do not see the links'. One solution, Jennifer offers, is to make cross-curricular links to history from other subjects. This is a solution to providing a context for work and making relevant and purposeful links across the curriculum. An example cited by Jennifer was that of the links between mathematics, science and history that are offered by studying the life and times of Sir Isaac Newton.

Among the group, responses regarding the approaches to teaching history were mixed. It seems that everyone was aware of the Ofsted ideal of discrete subject-specific lessons with a clear historical focus. However, from the responses elicited from this small panel, it would appear that links to other subjects are evident in planning and the thoughts of teachers and, in some cases, positively encouraged. In some cases, the time-table may clearly state that history is being taught; however, if relevant and valuable experiences for the children exist, then cross-curricular activities are positively sought out. Katie said that her school taught themes and that cross-curricular approaches were seen as advantageous as they helped provide a context for the learning. This included selecting texts for English that supported other subjects in the curriculum, such as *Stay Where You Are and Then Leave* by John Boyne, which supports work on the First World War, and *The Silver Sword* by Ian Serraillier, which supports work on the Second World War. This considered approach to cross-curricular work underlines the findings of the Primary History Survey (Jones, 2011) which indicated that most history teaching made good use of such approaches and could not be considered solely as discrete subject teaching. However, as we have seen, Ofsted's professional development materials indicate that effective teaching included 'thoughtful cross-curricular links which ensure that historical understanding is nurtured through other opportunities' (Ofsted, 2012).

The new curriculum was met positively by Jennifer, an NQT, and Emma and Martha, who are final-year trainees. They are generally happy with its structure and commented that it had clear expectations that clearly defined what to teach, although not necessarily how to teach it. Martha contemplated the challenges facing teachers and the teaching of history. She responded that the breadth of the curriculum could induce anxiety among teachers with less teaching experience as well as trainee teachers, especially where less familiar topics are concerned. The need for strong planning was also highlighted, as this solid scaffolding could overcome such anxieties. It is widely agreed that planning history, and developing secure subject knowledge is time-consuming but necessary. This is offset, in Martha's mind, by the sheer enthusiasm for teaching history that is so evident. Martha is keen to teach history and enjoys the process of planning lessons, organising trips and developing approaches for her lessons, such as role-play and, most importantly, enquiry using artefacts. These are principles that have been learned in university seminars and are now being put into practice.

The importance of dialogic talk is also highlighted by Martha, who recognises how discussions can lead to new questions and further investigations for the children to undertake. Thinking about the children's learning, Martha, reflects that the depth of understanding can be seen in their ability to consider people's attitudes back in time compared to now. This level of engagement highlights the understanding of history as being about not only subject knowledge but also the wider aspects of history, such as historical imagination. Martha also refers to the children's interest in and enthusiasm for finding out about the past as being one of the best things about teaching history. Martha's fear for history teaching is that there is too much of a focus on dates, facts and the need for children to remember them. When teaching chronological understanding, Martha is determined to create inspiring lessons that address the concept of chronology without simply dealing with dates and events. She is more confident in providing history lessons that deal with perspectives, historiography and different points of view. As a final-year trainee, it is pleasing that Martha recognises the benefits of other opportunities that teaching history can provide, such as learning outside the classroom (Department for Education and Skills, 2006) and developing the whole child through aspects of social, cultural, moral and religious considerations.

Planning history lessons for unfamiliar topics, such as ancient Sumer, initiates Martha's thoughts surrounding the challenges of teaching ancient history as opposed to the more 'accessible' recent past, a consideration for all concerned with the delivering the 2014 curriculum. As a final-year trainee, she is aware of the debate about discrete subject teaching versus a cross-curricular approach. At this stage in her career she has had little opportunity to choose which approach she prefers, but this awareness and an understanding of the pros and cons of each approach will stand her in good stead. She adds that other opportunities, such as investigating other eras, should be promoted much more in schools. While there might be logistical considerations as to why these opportunities are overlooked or limited, it is good that new teachers are recognising these gaps and are willing to try to fill them.

Emma, as a final-year trainee, adds that a lack of confidence when understanding pedagogic approaches in the delivery of history lessons could be a barrier to teaching the subject well. She worries about the value placed upon history in the primary school, stating that 'more needs to be done to enhance its significance'. This refers, of course, not only to history in school, but history in the budget, in the curriculum and on the timetable.

Katie, the deputy head, commented that, as a school manager, embedding the skills across both key stages was time-consuming and that ensuring that the aims of the curriculum were being met had been the main focus and challenge for her school, whilst accommodating and planning for the 'topics' in the 2014 curriculum, although also time-consuming, had been less of an issue.

A final thought from Katie, who enthused about the children's interest earlier: 'I love teaching history and I think the children's enthusiasm starts with the teacher. If they love it and get excited, the children will do too.' As regards to developing subject knowledge, Katie advocates that teachers, NQTs and trainee teachers all need to go to a good pub quiz!

For final-year trainees, much of our time in history specialism seminars is spent considering 'employability'. This means considering what makes a good teacher, what good history teaching is and how to put this into practice. Another aspect of this is that of the role of a subject manager or coordinator. As such, final-year trainees were given the opportunity to ask Laura, a history coordinator, questions about her role, history teaching and the management of the subject. In Table 8.3 Laura offers her advice for those with ambitions of becoming coordinators themselves as well as those with questions just about teaching history.

Table 8.3 Views from a history coordinator

Q. How do you make teaching history interactive and fun in the classroom?

The best type of history lesson is one which is hands-on and thought-provoking for the children. (Do you ever remember that worksheet where you filled in the missing gaps with words? No! But I bet you remember when your teacher brought in some artefacts to discover. Or when you had to act out a scene for history.)

Artefacts, enquiry, costumes, drama workshops – have a history day. Get your class (and yourself, of course) to dress up to follow your topic and complete your day in that style. For example, the Year 5 teacher in my school teaches the Victorians as part of the local study unit, and to celebrate the end of the topic he organises a Victorian school day by setting up a Victorian-style classroom in the hall – the children use slate and chalk, he uses a blackboard to teach. He also invites a drama workshop in to work with the children.

Another way to make history interesting is to invite people in to speak about your topic such as family members, especially if you are covering a topic on the local area.

Finally, and most obviously, school trips!

Q. How do teachers engage with teaching history?

Teachers enjoy teaching history just as the children enjoy learning about different topics. There are any number of approaches to use in the classroom, enquiry being the most prominent approach at the moment. Another reason why history is a great subject to teach is down to the cross-curricular possibilities. This makes history great for a teacher who can really make strong links across the curriculum and provide a great context for the learning. History is also great for upper Key Stage 2 where the main emphasis is on writing as it gives children a chance to learn something 'different' than to literacy, but, if the teacher wishes, to still apply literacy skills (e.g. report writing, stories, diaries).

Q. What is your biggest challenge and how do you deal with it?

Budget! Sadly, schools do not give history much money for budget, so what little amount you have has to be spent on resources for the whole school. Resources are also quite expensive! A way around this is to borrow project loans from the local library/authority. Some museums also loan out artefacts. If your budget allows, organising visitors – drama workshops are great and they bring all necessary equipment with them (and it may even be possible to 'borrow' money from another area such as literacy who always get a huge budget and claim it will help develop drama skills and speech and language skills!).

Q. Is there enough flexibility in the curriculum to cover things such as the First World War?

Simple answer, yes. There is some flexibility to introduce topics and teach additional eras, even if they do not appear directly in the curriculum. For instance, a couple of years ago, with such a milestone as the First World War centenary, the majority of schools incorporated work on the war, as this is such a crucial part of history.

For my school, I organised a whole-school First World War Remembrance Day. The children produced work across the curriculum including art, design technology and writing that featured in a display at the museum. It was a proud moment for the children.

Schools have the flexibility to go off timetable to celebrate significant times (e.g. multicultural weeks, Black history week), so this is a great time to cover unusual or additional topics that you may want to teach.

Q. What does your role as history coordinator entail from day to day but also in the long term?

Day to day, you need a solid knowledge of the curriculum and of the school's long-term plan. Knowing who is teaching what and when will help you on a day-to-day basis and help plan and cater for their needs as they arise. Being one step ahead is a good plan, that way you can help your colleagues when they come and ask for help for ideas, trips and anything else that might arise.

In some ways, the start of the academic year and the end are the busiest periods. You will be involved in planning meetings and audits at these times. In between, you will also be managing the budget. This is specifically money to spend on history resources. So, talking to your colleagues about their plans for history for the future is really important. You usually budget up to a year ahead.

In the long term, you will need to create a long-term overview for each year group and each key stage. This will help ensure that the national curriculum is being covered. In addition to this, you need to map out the skills across the key stages, so that it is clear when children will be visiting different approaches and that, again, they are being met.

Contacts are useful too. Museums, education staff, parents and outside agencies will all be useful in promoting history in your school.

Q. How difficult do you find it to make history enjoyable to teachers who have a negative view of the subject?

In my experience, most teachers enjoy teaching history as it is so interactive and the children do enjoy learning about it, especially topics such as the Egyptians and the Romans. It is also a great subject to engage boys in and get good pieces of writing. So people can see other advantages to the subject.

History is also a good subject to engage all types of learners, and it can be a really creative subject too. Children can create posters, reports, film responses – share their ideas in a variety of ways and using different methods. So I think this helps teachers who aren't necessarily historical too.

Maybe some teachers do see history as a 'filler' subject – something to do for an hour on a Tuesday afternoon. In these instances, there are opportunities for CPD, subject-led staff meetings and whole-school theme days that will help those teachers to see the potential history has to develop independent thinkers and to challenge their ideas. It is up to the history coordinators to show those types of teachers the benefit teaching history has for children and how history will develop skills in other subjects too.

Q. What sort of duties do you have?

I manage the history budget and order resources for each year group. I also create a long-term overview for each key stage (and individual year groups if necessary). I ensure all teachers know the curriculum and share the long-term plan with them. I'll update teachers on any changes made to the national curriculum or any initiatives or events that I want the school to be involved in.

In addition to ordering resources, I help teachers locate any additional resources they may require to help teach a topic (e.g. by using project loans).

I provide the school with opportunities to participate in any local or national history schemes or events. When requested by the head teacher, I also do learning walks to observe the teaching of history throughout the school.

Q. Does your school teach history as a subject lesson or just part of a topic?

My school teaches history as a subject in its own right but as we do follow a creative curriculum, we will try to link topics into other subjects where possible to help children establish links between subjects and to encourage them to use their skills developed in other areas/subjects into other lessons they use (e.g. use their literacy skills in their history, RE or science lesson).

I think it is important to use only clear links between subjects if teaching a topic and not to try to force links just to say it is cross-curricular (e.g. don't teach Roman numerals in maths just because you are teaching Romans in history!)

Q. What approaches to teaching history do you use?

I use artefacts. Sometimes I use replica artefacts which can be ordered online. These help gain children's interests and develop questioning skills.

An idea would be to put a selection of items on a table and question cards such as what is this?, what is it used for?, what does it do? what material is it made from?, how old is it? This will get the children thinking, predicting and using logic and their ideas to answer questions.

Of course, if you did this every lesson, it would become dull and so you need to use a range of approaches.

You can also have drama workshops visit or visit museums.

Think about the communication aspect. What are the children going to make or do? They could make a book, video or podcast detailing all of the information they have learnt. This would be a good outcome of their learning at the end of a lesson or topic.

Q. How do you make history fun without the use of resources and artefacts?

Although history is more interesting when using items to physically explore, it is still possible to teach a good lesson without artefacts. It is best to stay away from worksheets – children will not enjoy them or remember them come next week!

History is a great subject which allows lots of questioning, discovery and researching. Children love to find out information for themselves or in groups, so set them up in groups and challenge them to find out more information on a specific area of your topic. For example, if teaching Egyptians, set up four groups and each group has to find out information about a different area: the pyramids; the pharaohs; gods; and life in ancient Egypt. Give children access to tablets/computers/books to research and make sure children allocate roles in their groups to ensure purposeful research (e.g. researcher, scribe, leader). Give children a time limit for them to gather information and then produce a poster to share information gathered and feed back to the class. Children have then taken ownership of their own learning.

Q. How do you track progress in history across both key stages?

It is up to individual teachers to track the progress of their class in history. There are plenty of tracking sheets available online, and it is also quite simple to devise your own methods of tracking to assess if learning objectives have been achieved.

It is possible to track progress via completing work scrutiny. This can be undertaken as part of a lesson observation and by looking through samples of books from lower-, middle- and higher-ability children in each class. Sometimes this is a focus for a staff meeting.

Q. How do you plan at Key Stage 1?

The national curriculum states what topics need to be covered in each key stage and also what elements are statutory and non-statutory. Some of the topics in Key Stage 1 are very open and can be adopted to suit a topic being taught and help support ideas in other subjects. For example, in our Year 1 class the teacher was teaching a topic about bridges. She got the class to design and make bridges using various resources in DT and tested the strength of them. They made different sized bridges and measured them using different units of measurements (maths). They discovered what materials were best to use (science) and even where famous bridges were located around the world (geography). To link this topic to history she focused on lives of significant individuals in the past who have contributed to national and international achievements, and taught her class about Isambard Kingdom Brunel.

Q. How do you plan at Key Stage 2?

At Key Stage 2 the children revisit skills that they will have already encountered in Key Stage 1. However, this is matched to the purpose of the curriculum and the aims of the curriculum to ensure that the children are addressing all the intended experiences.

Schemes of work are written around enquiry-based learning and the use of artefacts in lessons. Some lessons will start with a research question in mind, whilst other lessons will allow the children to develop their own lines of enquiry.

A range of teaching and learning experiences are planned. These include theme days, learning outside the classroom opportunities and visitors coming into school. We also try to provide a balance between 'doing history' and 'knowledge'.

A range of sources of information are used in other lessons in order to provide different perspectives of the past.

Summary

This chapter has considered approaches towards developing our own understanding and confidence as well as providing support for lesson observations and planning. The opinions, ideas and thoughts of several professionals at various stages in their careers have also been offered as a means of considering the teaching of history, the implementation of the 2014 curriculum and putting theory into practice.

References

Davies, J. and Redmond, J. (2005) *Coordinating History across the Primary School*. London: Fulton.

Department for Education (2013a) *Teachers' Standards*. London: DfE.

Department for Education (2013b) *The National Curriculum for England*. London: DfE.

Department for Education and Skills (2006) *Learning Outside the Classroom Manifesto*. Nottingham: DfES.

Jones, M. (2011) What history should we teach? The teachers' perspective: The Historical Association's Primary Survey. *Primary History* 57.

Ofsted (2011) *History for All*. Manchester: Ofsted.

Ofsted (2012) *Ofsted's Subject Professional Development Materials: History*. Manchester: Ofsted.

9
A primary history toolkit

Children encounter historical concepts and thoughts in all manner of places and, as we have seen, historical details, facts and figures, can be the starting point that captures a child's imagination and motivates them to find out more about the past. This chapter sets out to harness that enjoyment and enthusiasm for history and to think about the lessons and activities that we design in the primary school.

In preparing this book, I reflected upon the type of book I wanted it to be. I knew it was imperative to set out the importance of a deep understanding of the discipline of history and for readers to have an understanding of the specific subject attributes of history. I also wanted the book to clearly set out the aspects of history and convey the importance of addressing historical skills, concepts and attitudes and values as well as developing an awareness of the importance of the content of history and the process of history within our history teaching.

Another aim of the book was to highlight the importance of history and the value of history in the primary school. I wanted to reflect upon the current position of the subject, while also considering the context within which we are working.

One theme running throughout the book is that of a practical toolkit of ideas for you to readily implement and build upon. I have already included some toolkit ideas in previous chapters in order to provide some examples both to support the discussion and to get you started in your primary history teaching. The toolkit ideas are designed to support you and to boost your confidence in planning your own topics and delivering your own history lessons. To conclude the book, then, this chapter contains a further bank of toolkit ideas to enhance your teaching of primary history, whether you are a trainee teacher, NQT or early career teacher.

As identified in Chapter 8, planning for history teaching and developing subject knowledge can be time-consuming, even if ultimately highly rewarding. You need to manage your time effectively in order to develop your subject knowledge and ensure that it is deep enough to plan and deliver purposeful lessons that challenge the children and develop historical skills, concepts, and attitudes and values. Further, you need deep subject knowledge in order to plan effectively. My fear is that the temptation for busy teachers, with little time and long to-do lists, is to fall back on time-filler activities, internet lessons, or the latest gimmick. This does not do justice to the subject and strays from the ideals of good primary history teaching that have been set out in these pages. Therefore these toolkit ideas, although not an end solution in themselves, are intended as a guiding hand on a long journey. They contain a clear focus upon the aspects of history and ensure that both the content and process of history are being addressed. While there can never be a quick fix through top teacher tips, this section is designed to provide starting points and ideas for classroom practice. Many trainees have indicated that such a practical starting point towards classroom activities boosts their confidence in planning and helps them learn to deliver good focused history sessions in school.

Every toolkit idea included here can be adapted to suit the more specific needs of your class in terms of age, ability, special educational needs/disability, English as an additional language and other factors that influence the teaching of your lessons with your class. In some instances, the specific key stage for a particular toolkit idea will be clear based upon the topic and activity that is age appropriate. These toolkit ideas arise from the 'three-lens approach' for teaching the foundation subjects as advocated by Webster and Misra (2015).

Toolkit idea 9.1

Place names

Aspects of history: Legacy, evidence

This investigation is commonly associated with units on the Anglo-Saxons, Vikings and Romans who all left clues as to their settlements throughout Britain. One way of presenting this in a primary school is to investigate maps and, having shared common place name endings, challenge the children to find examples on their maps. This will undoubtedly involve discussing the meanings of the place name endings, which may cast a light on the landscape or land use in the past, providing an indication of the geography of your locality in the past and the activities that were carried out there in the past.

Toolkit idea 9.2

How great was Alfred?

Aspects of history: Interpretation, evidence, validity of evidence, enquiry

Challenge the children to explore the life, times and achievements of Alfred the Great, using a range of sources and comparing Alfred's reign to those who reigned before and after him. Through this investigation children can explore interpretations of Alfred the Great, as well as being encouraged to sift arguments and weigh evidence in order to come to their conclusions. This approach can be used when investigating any historical figure. Posing the enquiry as a question may motivate the children to prove or disprove a theory or belief, while adding a sense of purpose to the investigation itself. Time permitting, it would be interesting to investigate other people from the past with reputations, such as King John, whose legacy may be tainted by the stories of Robin Hood, or Marie Antoinette, who is often depicted as a socialite. While these people may not appear in the curriculum, the process of history adopted in order to find out about them does address elements of the national curriculum.

Toolkit idea 9.3

What does the Sutton Hoo discovery tell us about Anglo-Saxon people?

Aspects of history: Enquiry, change, continuity, interpretation, weighing evidence

Acting as archaeologists, challenge the children to investigate the Sutton Hoo discoveries and consider what the findings imply about the lives of Anglo-Saxon people and their beliefs. This can be done through photographs of the artefacts found at the site and a line of enquiry from the teacher that asks the children to interpret what they can see and what this implies about Anglo-Saxon life. This style of interrogation of an artefact can be conducted with almost any item from any age. Each new question challenges the children to think a little bit more and to unveil a new level to their thinking, helping them to make links and connections and to piece together a picture of the past.

Toolkit idea 9.4

Who is Tim Berners-Lee?

Aspects of history: Enquiry, influence, impact, change, legacy, evidence

Challenge the children to create a fact file based upon information provided and prepared by the class teacher. This will help address your own subject knowledge as well as aid in the creation of an information pack that the children will use in order to find out information about the life and work of Tim Berners-Lee. Emphasis can be placed upon innovation and impact of Tim's work, especially with a view to using this as part of the suggested investigation in the curriculum in comparing the lives and times of Tim Berners-Lee and William Caxton. Therefore, a similar information pack could be prepared on William Caxton.

Toolkit idea 9.5

Tiachtli

Aspects of history: Enquiry, change, continuity, legacy, interpretation

This activity explores the ancient game of Tiachtli and fits into the study of a non-European society, in this case, the Aztecs. Tiachtli was a tennis-like game, although no racquets were used, and it was played on a court-shaped like a capital letter 'I'. The players scored a goal by putting a ball through carved stone rings. Points were also awarded for style and skill. Comparisons between this game and modern alternatives such as rugby and football can be made and, in addition, children can compare reporting on the game using the reference from Diego Durán, who was a Dominican friar—'On seeing the ball come at them, as it was about to touch the floor, the players were so quick to turn their knees or buttocks to the ball they returned it with extraordinary swiftness. With this bouncing back and forth they suffered terrible injuries on their knees and thighs' (Noble, 2012: 148)—and a current sports correspondent describing a passage of play in a modern game of football. Further research could be conducted to find out more about Aztec pastimes and make further comparisons between the two cultures and times.

Toolkit idea 9.6

Board games

Aspects of history: Change, continuity, enquiry

Another way in which societies of the past can be explored is through their pastimes. This could be developed through the chronological study strand of the 2014 national curriculum, challenging the children to find out about board games and pastimes of the past. This could include exploring Viking games, such as hnefatafl, or the associated Anglo-Saxon game of taefl. Societies that have developed strategy games that appear to be similar in nature to chess, draughts and solitaire can be explored, as can Tudor board games, including backgammon and nine men's morris. The history of chess can be explored, as can games from earlier times such as senet from the Ancient Egyptian era.

Toolkit idea 9.7

Haiku

Aspect of history: Subject knowledge

This is a fun means of developing subject knowledge among the class. The traditional Japanese poem form of three lines with a strict 5–7–5 syllable structure challenges the children to think carefully about a topic of study in history. The poems themselves are not too complicated to detract from the history work taking place and can be used as a form of assessment if the teacher chooses to adopt a triangulation approach to assessment. Final outcomes will provide an insight into the children's understanding of a unit of study. The haiku can be used to focus the children in their thinking as to a particular artefact that is associated with a topic, specific event or person from the past. Used in conjunction with other forms of assessment, haiku can be an enjoyable way of exploring a topic.

Toolkit idea 9.8

Acrostic poems

Aspect of history: Subject knowledge

As with the haiku, acrostic poems serve as a fun and interesting way for the children to demonstrate their subject knowledge of a topic, artefact or historical figure or event. The focus here is upon the historical element of their work. The acrostic poem itself should not need too much introduction, leaving the children free to create interesting poems about their given item or event. While there may be strong cross-curricular links to English with these toolkit ideas, the important thing to remember is that we are looking for ways of engaging the children's interest and developing their historical knowledge and understanding. Seasoned practitioners will know that intriguing classroom approaches will enhance a unit rather than detract from it.

Toolkit idea 9.9

Origami book

Aspects of history: Subject knowledge, enquiry

Teachers with an interest in Design Technology will know that the idea of an origami book can be used to create fantastic pieces of work with countless flaps to lift, tags to pull and pop-up elements. Children enjoy creating such pieces, and through such work their creativity is allowed to develop and shine. Origami books, even simple versions without any flaps, tags or pop-up features, provide a simple way for the children to record their subject knowledge on a topic or to create a fact file exploring a certain element of their work, with, for example, each page representing a different Greek god or goddess. Research into the topic or unit that is being covered will also be conducted in order for the children to find the subject knowledge to include in their books. As with haiku and acrostic poems, the focus must be maintained upon the historical objectives of the lesson rather than the DT skills required. However, there is nothing to stop the book being created over two different subject lessons.

Toolkit idea 9.10

Food through the ages

Aspect of history: Chronology, enquiry

This project would require children to explore the diets of people of the past. This would again fit nicely into a chronological study unit at Key Stage 2 where children could investigate how technology has altered farming methods and the processes involved in the food industry and therefore the food we eat, as well as the eating habits and food that people ate in the past. Additional investigations could consider the difference between the diets of rich and poor people at various times in the past as well as the crockery and utensils associated with food at those times. The impact of rationing could be investigated with a view to researching the nutrition and diet of wartime children and that of children today. Discussion here might lead to work in other curriculum areas such as PSCHE and PE.

Toolkit idea 9.11

How do we find out about the past?

Aspects of history: Process of history, enquiry, evidence

The 2014 curriculum for Key Stages 1 and 2 makes mention of the ways in which we find out about the past. This refers directly to the process of history, as highlighted earlier in this book. The question 'how do we find out about the past?' can be tackled in different ways according to the age of your class and their previous experiences. Children could be asked to gather togther as many ideas as they can about finding out about the past; the answers are then collected by going around the class, table by table or individually, collating scores along the lines of TV's *Pointless* game show where low-scoring answers win. The focus, of course, is upon the range of methods employed by historians in order to piece together a picture of the past. Discussions here will no doubt explore the validity of sources as well as the nature and reliability of sources.

Toolkit idea 9.12

We will remember them

Aspects of history: Cultures, traditions, subject knowledge, enquiry, representations of the past, interpretations of the past

Using a British Legion poppy as an artefact for this lesson, teachers can initiate a discussion about symbols and their meanings. This could be done through looking at other symbols that are familiar to the children, such as a yellow M and a Nike swoosh, as well as less familiar symbols such as a Christian fish, a green cross to represent a chemist shop, traffic signs and potentially the symbolism included in your school badge. Discussion from these starting points can then lead to the significance of poppies, their association with remembrance and the tradition of wearing a poppy in the weeks leading up to Armistice Day. Another aspect of this toolkit idea, of course, is that, to some people, the poppy has other associations and is not worn at all. This would allow discussions to examine the fact that different versions of the past can exist.

Toolkit idea 9.13

Egyptian daze

Aspects of history: Enquiry, subject knowledge, change, continuity, learning outside the curriculum

This toolkit idea can be considered as a starting point for a topic upon the ancient Egyptians, whereby the life and times of the ancient Egyptians can be explored as aspects of everyday life in Egyptian times. This could include everything from the food of the ancient Egyptians to the clothes that they wore. Children can explore Egyptian technology, the importance of the River Nile to the lives of ancient Egyptian people, medicine, homes, pastimes, farming, as well as beliefs, the afterlife and gods and goddesses. In this unit, there should also be an acknowledgement of the changes over time within the timeframe of the ancient Egyptians themselves, in that ancient Egyptian fashions, for instance, would not have been the same at the start of the era as they were at the end. Activities in this field could incorporate research using a range of sources, and the potential for field trips to suitable museums with an egyptology focus, such as Liverpool World Museum.

Toolkit idea 9.14

Who would live in a Stone Age house like this?

Aspects of history: Enquiry, evidence, change, continuity, subject knowledge

In investigating aspects of history, such as change and continuity, children can explore similarities and differences within the houses of the three eras of the unit. From caves to huts, children can investigate the houses of the period and features that they have in common, such as designated places for fires and cooking, beds and storage. Children can also explore the materials that were used to build and furnish homes, such as wood and animal hides.

Toolkit idea 9.15

Cave paintings

Aspects of history: Enquiry, interpretations, change

Investigating what cave paintings tell us and where they have been found would form an interesting aspect of a Stone Age study. Cave paintings often depicted everyday things such as hunting animals, harvesting and cooking. The cave paintings at Lascaux are estimated to be around 17,300 years old and depict animals that roamed the Dordogne at the time, while similar cave paintings have been found across Europe, providing evidence of Stone Age people and their settlements and movements. This would also present an opportunity to discuss the possible interpretations as to why such paintings were created and a comparison with the ways in which we communicate our ideas, record our thoughts and share with others.

Toolkit idea 9.16

Timeline of historical vocabulary

Aspects of history: Historical vocabulary, chronology

At both Key Stages 1 and 2, children are encouraged to engage with historical vocabulary. This can include historical vocabulary referring to specific events, such as 'armistice', 'revolt', 'rebellion' or 'resistance', and terms referring to the passing of time, such as 'century', 'medieval', 'modern', 'prehistoric', 'decade', 'BC', 'AD' and 'BCE'. Children could be challenged to place such terms in chronological order, in order to further develop an understanding of chronology and a sense of the passing of time as well as a sense of depth of time.

Toolkit idea 9.17

Choosing and using (Key Stage 1)

Aspects of history: Evidence, enquiry, validity of sources

The title of this toolkit idea refers to the phrase 'choosing and using parts of a story' that appears in the Key Stage 1 national curriculum. The actual topic to be studied could come from any area of the Key Stage 1 curriculum. However, in addressing this idea of choosing and using, it is not difficult to imagine the children being presented with a range of source materials, perhaps to do with their locality study. Here, anecdotal accounts may conflict with written records or with the oral accounts of others. In this case, the children will need to make decisions, based upon the evidence before them, as to what they feel is the most reliable of the sources. It also acts as an introduction to the idea that more than one version of the past may exist and allows children the opportunity to investigate reasons as to why this may be the case.

Toolkit idea 9.18

Changes in national life

Aspect of history: Subject knowledge, significant events, legacy, cultural understanding

The national curriculum makes reference to the children's studies considering changes in national life. To some, this will provide an opportunity for classroom studies to explore the world wars. Most towns and villages have a war memorial and this could be used as a starting point for lessons that explore the impact the world wars had on their local area and on national life. At Key Stage 1, such a study could also fall under the 'events beyond living memory that are significant nationally or globally'. With no specific mention of either world war within the curriculum for Key Stages 1 and 2, teachers will still feel that studying this aspect of the past is a valuable element of children's historical understanding. Through opportunities such as this, and through studying the significance of poppies, studying the world wars can remain an important part of the school curriculum.

Toolkit idea 9.19

The Great Fire of London

Aspects of history: Subject knowledge, change, evidence

A staple of the curriculum for some time, the Great Fire of London is also referred to in the 2014 curriculum, which means that many teachers will have approached this topic from a variety of angles over the years. We can look at the events that led to the fire using accounts, such as Samuel Pepys's reference to it in his diaries, as well as looking at the rate of spread of the fire across London's wooden infrastructure. We can also look at the outbreak of the fire at Thomas Farriner's bakery on Pudding Lane and the maid who became one of the few victims of the fire. In building up this subject knowledge, the opportunity to investigate the sequence of events arises. Here, children can be challenged to sequence the events of the Great Fire of London in chronological order, thereby developing chronological understanding as well as subject knowledge.

There are opportunities to look at the Great Fire through reports, accounts, maps and other sources. Such an approach would not only address subject knowledge, but also provide opportunities for the children to engage with change, and using evidence.

Toolkit idea 9.20

Who was Emily Davison?

Aspect of history: Subject knowledge, significant individuals

This toolkit idea can be adapted to any significant person whom you choose to study with your class. Emily Davison is referred to in the Key

Stage 1 national curriculum, and is part of a suggested comparison unit, comparing the life and achievements of Emily Davison with those of Rosa Parks. Both women have come to represent the causes they stood for. This study also allows for the children to study the times of the people they are studying as well as their lives. The children can be challenged to compile fact files about such significant people, making a note of comparable features of their lives as well as specific details about their individual lives. Emily Davison is probably best known for two events in her life. Firstly, for hiding in a cupboard in St Mary Undercroft, the chapel of the Palace of Westminster, on the night of 2 April 1911, in order to legitimately claim that her residence, on the 1911 Census, was the House of Commons. This is an event that is today commemorated with a plaque at the House of Commons. The second event was the incident that led to Davison's death in 1913. Davison attended the 1913 Epsom Derby and ran onto the course as the King's horse, Anmer, approached the run-in. The subsequent collision knocked the jockey, Herbert Jones, unconscious, caused Anmer to somersault and killed Davison herself. It is thought that Davison was trying to attach a suffragette flag to Anmer's bridle in order to further publicise the cause to which Davison is most closely associated. Film of the event does exist through Pathé news reels. While you may think twice about sharing such evidence with younger children, given the nature of what happens, it is an interesting source in developing your own subject knowledge, which is, of course, an important aspect of your own development and engagement with history.

Toolkit idea 9.21

Iron Age fort

Aspect of history: Historical imagination, subject knowledge, chronological understanding, evidence

In developing historical imagination, it is essential to provide opportunities for the children to immerse themselves in the eras and times of their study. When studying 'changes in Britain from the Stone Age to the Iron Age' the children can explore Iron Age hill forts, their locations in Britain and the interpretations as to these sites' existence. For instance, some are believed to have been built as fortresses, while some mark settlements and others mark religious sites and ceremonies. Historical imagination can be developed here by questioning the children about what they think it would have been like to live in a hill fort. Understanding of Iron Age forts can be further extended through the use of online resources such as the

British Museum[1] and BBC History. Through resources such as these, sites such as Maiden Castle offer a possible chronological study of the site from its Iron Age origins through to its occupation by the Romans in Britain. Today, the site of Maiden Castle is maintained by English Heritage[2] and is open to the public and school visits.

[1]http://www.britishmuseum.org
[2]http://www.english-heritage.org.uk

Toolkit idea 9.22

Why did the Romans invade Britain?

Aspects of history: Subject knowledge, reasoning, informed responses, weigh evidence, sift arguments

The Romans invaded Britain three times between 55 BC and AD 43. The first two invasions led by Julius Caesar within a year may be considered more as reconnaissance missions establishing possible trade links as well as including skirmishes with Celtic tribes. The Romans under Caesar established that Britain offered a prestigious gain for the Roman Empire as well as other benefits such as slaves, fertile land and raw materials including iron, lead, zinc, copper, silver and gold. The third invasion in AD 43, under Emperor Claudius, was designed not only to capitalise on the raw materials Britain had to offer, but also as a show of strength to the rest of the Empire in continuing the tradition of claiming new territories. Romans, it is thought, believed that it was their duty to conquer new parts of the world in order to spread their civilisation. This offers possible comparisons with British imperialism hundreds of years later. In addition to the general show of power and strength the invasion brought, Emperor Claudius had other reasons for conquering new territories under his own name, as he had only recently become Emperor and wanted to establish his own ambition. Another consideration is that the final invasion of Britain by the Romans could be seen as revenge as the Britons had offered support to the Gauls (French).

Children could be challenged to sort reasons for the invasions, perhaps with some feasible red herrings thrown in. This would enable the children to provide explanations and rationales as to the invasions. In this way, children are engaged with aspects of the Key Stage 2 national curriculum such as 'constructing informed responses that involve thoughtful selection and organisation of relevant historical information' (DFE, 2013).

Toolkit idea 9.23

Life on the Wall

Aspects of history: Historical imagination, subject knowledge, change and continuity, learning outside the classroom, evidence

While exploring Roman Britain, lessons will undoubtedly include investigating Hadrian's Wall. This could be done through investigating living conditions for soldiers at Housesteads Roman Fort, an English Heritage site that was originally called 'Vercovicium', which meant 'the place of the effective fighters'. This translation could be used as a starting point for the investigation of the Wall, the need for the Wall and a Roman soldier's life on the Wall.

Vindolanda, an auxiliary fort just south of Hadrian's Wall, offers further insight into the life of a soldier at the boundaries of the Empire. The museum and archaeological sites offer opportunities for learning outside the classroom, but for those for whom such a field trip would be logistically challenging, the website offers resources and activities that would enable children to develop their understanding of this area. Vindolanda is probably most famed for the discovery of the 'Vindolanda tablets'. These are the oldest known handwritten documents in Britain. They consist of postcard-sized pieces of wood with ink handwriting. There are around 752 tablets in total, although new tablets are being discovered all the time. Many of these tablets are on display at the British Museum. This could be developed within lessons as a study of change and continuity of everyday aspects of life (in this case, writing). Translated tablets can be used to discuss the content and what insight this offers as to the lives of the soldiers. Comparisons with today could be developed, with children exploring the kind of occasions on which we write and the messages we write and send to one another today.

Toolkit idea 9.24

What was Roman Britain like?

Aspect of history: Enquiry, subject knowledge, weigh evidence

Posing a question often provides an opening for classroom discussions. Here, children need to compile their subject knowledge as to life in Britain during Roman times. Children can work in groups in order to investigate different aspects of Roman life using a range of source materials that may include replica artefacts, electronic sources and media clips and documentaries. The children can then bring all their ideas together, in a similar vein to Paul Ginnis's (2002) 'Marketplace' activity, in order to produce a collaborative piece of work.

The question may be rephrased to ask the children whether they would like to live in Roman Britain and to provide an explanation for their choice. In this way, children are again engaging with elements of the national curriculum that go beyond just subject knowledge.

Toolkit idea 9.25

Were the Vikings violent?

Aspects of history: Challenging stereotypes, evidence, representations of the past, place names, legacy

This toolkit idea uses the *Horrible Histories* Simon and Garfunkel spoof where the stereotypical image of Vikings as being violent is challenged. As part of their studies, the children can explore the evidence and decide whether the image of marauding raiders is a fair summary of the Vikings in Britain and as a people as a whole. This could lead to work on stereotypes and representations of the past. There is also the opportunity to include an investigation of place names and their meanings, some of which are referred to in the *Horrible Histories* Simon and Garfunkel song.

Toolkit idea 9.26

Benin

Aspects of history: Subject knowledge, evidence, interpretation, legacy

As a perhaps overlooked aspect of the national curriculum, the BBC Bitesize web pages provide a useful starting point for the study of Benin at Key Stage 2, dividing the unit into seven key areas.[3] These include investigating the kingdom of Benin, how the kingdom began, locating Benin, the transformation from a kingdom to an empire, trade and the decline of the empire, as well as the legacy. Individual teachers can supplement these starting points by adding their own ideas and areas of investigation. These could include utilising the sources available through the British Museum web pages as well as other sources that can be found on the web. In order to develop specific historical skills and concepts, teachers could

[3]http://www.bbc.co.uk/guides/z3n7mp3

encourage their children to make comparisons between Benin and other parts of the world at the same time, as well as the potential exploration of artefacts, through photographs and the inferences and judgements that can be drawn from these sources of evidence.

Toolkit idea 9.27

The Indus Valley

Aspect of history: Subject knowledge, evidence, interpretation

The Indus Valley is often overlooked in order for schools to accommodate the more familiar ancient Egyptians. However, study of the Indus Valley offers the opportunity to develop historical subject knowledge of another civilisation as well as geographical links to the region. As with the study of other ancient civilisations, comparisons can be made between different eras and with modern life. However, perhaps more interestingly, the lack of evidence about the Indus Valley means that there are a lot of unanswered questions. Reputable sources, such as the BBC, provide some subject knowledge and details regarding the civilisation. This information can be treated in the same way as other history units in the primary classroom. Posing the question 'how do we find out about the Indus Valley?' will encourage the children to focus upon evidence, sources and interpretations of history, again using sources such as the British Museum.

Toolkit idea 9.28

Personal histories

Aspects of history: Personal histories, identity

We have discovered how history can be seen as existing in different forms, such as local history, family history and black history. One such strand of history is that of personal histories. These can be explored through looking at outside influences that form our ideas about the world. This relates to Cooper's (2012) 'Me' model as well as wider themes of identity.

An interesting way to approach this in the classroom is to use the poems of Michael Rosen that deal with his childhood memories, such as 'Chocolate Cake', 'The Watch' and 'Washing Up'. From sharing these poems, discussion can move to the children's own memories and experiences. There is an obvious cross-curricular link with English, which would see the children considering their own formative experiences in the form of a poem, but equally, this could be investigated through other forms of writing.

Toolkit idea 9.29

Who, what, when and why

Aspects of history: Interpretation, evidence, critical thinking

The curriculum refers to 'inspiring pupils' curiosity' and this, as we have seen, can be achieved in many ways. One way is through the use of photographs that can be used not only to engage the children's interest and curiosity, but also to develop historical intrigue in asking 'who, what, when and why?'. Images that depict famous events or just everyday images can stimulate discussion and interest. Banks of such photographs can be found through English Heritage's Heritage Explorer website.[4] These images can be coupled with images of startling events, such as Charles Godfloy flying through the Arc de Triomphe in 1919. Discussions that arise from looking at such images will address ideas of critical thinking and the use of evidence, especially if images are selected that raise issues of validity, such as Second World War propaganda photographs that are arguably designed to raise morale and keep people calm.

[4] http://www.heritage-explorer.co.uk/web/he/default.aspx

Toolkit idea 9.30

Sequencing

Aspects of history: Sequencing, chronology, critical thinking, rationale, explanations

A simple activity to address chronology and historical skills is that of sequencing a set of similar artefacts. In seminars, we use old cameras to sort and sequence. We discuss features of the cameras and then place them in order with a clear rationale. This activity could be done with items such as irons and telephones or indeed a set of any other household artefacts, including packaging of well-known brands, mobile phones and clocks. The children can be encouraged to discuss the sequence they decide upon and provide an explanation as to their thinking.

Toolkit idea 9.31

Dig it, man

Aspects of history: Enquiry, interpretation, evidence

Children can further their investigations, enquiries and understanding as to how we find out about the past through experiencing an archaeological dig. I've seen some schools conduct archaeological digs on their school field that have led to 'discoveries' enabling the children to piece together a picture of the past. In other cases, schools have used archaeological dig sets that are available for schools to purchase in order for schools to provide such experiences. In these cases, planted objects, and fragments of objects, are uncovered by the children, who brush them down and deduce the origins of the pieces they have found. This allows the children to apply their interpretations and consider several aspects of history, such as enquiry, interpretation, and the concept of evidence. The children are encouraged to record and photograph their findings in the same way as real archaeologists do. In this way, the children are working as real historians.

Toolkit idea 9.32

Was Napoleon short?

Aspects of history: Representations of the past, bias, propaganda, change and continuity

This toolkit idea challenges the children to consider how people are portrayed and the reasons for this. In this case, the children can consider how Napoleon, the leader of a rival nation, France, was portrayed (and is still portrayed) in popular culture. Contemporary magazines and newspapers depicted Napoleon as short at the time of his command of the French. However, was this a fair representation or media manipulation and a systematic undermining a foreign leader? The children can research this, using cartoons, newspapers and images of Napoleon that appeared at the time. Napoleon stood at 5 ft 6 in., which was taller than the national average of a Frenchman at the time (5 ft 4 in.). Nelson, the British Naval strategist, was 5 ft 4 in., while Wellington was taller, at 5 ft 9 in. This could lead to the children questioning the representations of historical figures and the reasons behind these images. Comparisons with contemporary figures and other adversaries of the past could be investigated, and, in doing so, children will address concepts of change and continuity as well as representations of the past.

Toolkit idea 9.33

Who lives in a house like this?

Aspects of history: Enquiry, evidence, interpretation, change, continuity

While investigating the locality, a topic of work that could potentially occur in planning for Key Stages 1 and 2 is that of a local street enquiry.

Census materials are currently available up to 1911. This means that children can investigate the people, families and occupations of their immediate locality. This interaction with hard evidence allows the children to deal with data and interpretations as they piece together the locality from over 100 years ago. There is also the opportunity to compare the street with another census year as well as the present day. The directions in which this enquiry could go are almost limitless and depend very much upon the specific findings of your enquiry. However, emerging themes may determine lines of enquiry that you wish to pursue. For instance, the average age of householders, the term 'head' when referring to the male occupant, as well as comparisons regarding domestic servants, lodgers, boarders, family units and the number of people living in each house. Opportunities then arise in investigating the year in more detail, widening the research from an investigation that considers one neighbourhood to considering what life was like in Britain in 1911. Everyday information, such as who was on the throne, who was prime minister and what happened in 1911, that has direct comparisons with today, can be investigated. Further comparisons between 1911 and today can be made in terms of the population of the country and life expectancy, while comparisons of pastimes, entertainment and news stories can add to the details of the investigation. Enquiries regarding census materials also allow for cross-curricular opportunities. One such opportunity could be for the children to create representations of houses and models of the buildings, complete with the relevant data for each house along the street. The focus must remain historical while allowing for other subjects to contribute to a more creative approach to the teaching of history.

Final thoughts

Over the course of this book, we have set out to examine primary history in our schools in light of the 2014 curriculum and recent reports outlining the teaching of history in primary schools.

Practical classroom toolkit ideas have been offered alongside a more considered and thoughtful examination of the subject of history and the value the subject has within schools.

A historical context has also been explored mapping out the long and winding journey of the subject of history in the context of primary education and its place in the current curriculum.

On this journey, history has been seen to be a versatile subject that offers opportunities for lessons to address a wealth of curriculum links as well as the specific aspects of history that are so important to the uniqueness of the subject of history. This point is of particular relevance. It is clear that Ofsted advocates a discrete subject approach to the teaching of history; however, evidence suggests that schools adopt an approach that combines subjects. This allows teachers to combine elements from across the entire curriculum, enabling children to assimilate their knowledge and understanding from a number of disciplines and produce pieces of work that convey their knowledge in new and interesting ways. Of course, it is important to stress that the integrity of the subject of history remains intact. This brings us back to the key message of this book, that of the importance of a deep understanding of what history is. Our teachers, trainee teachers and NQTs are responsible for accommodating the aspects of history within their schemes of work. Understanding that history is made up of historical skills, concepts, and attitudes and values and that these are delivered within lessons through a balance of the content of history and the process of history is essential.

References

Cooper, H. (2012) *History 5–11. A Guide for Teachers*. Abingdon: Routledge.

Department for Education (2013) *The National Curriculum for England*. London: DfE.

Ginnis, P. (2002) *The Teacher's Toolkit: Raise Classroom Achievement with Strategies for Every Learner*. Carmarthen: Crown House Publishing.

Noble, P. (2012) *The Primary Teacher's Guide to History*. London: Scholastic.

Webster, M. and Misra, S. (eds) (2015) *Teaching the Primary Foundation Subjects*. Maidenhead: Open University Press.

Index